BAD AT WORK

THE DYSFUNCTIONAL SH*T AND HOW TO GET PAST IT

TANYA RHONE

BAD AT WORK: *The Dysfunctional Sh*t and How to Get Past It*

Text Copyright © 2017 by Tanya Rhone
All rights reserved.

The use of any part of this publication reproduced, stored in any retrieval system, or transmitted in any forms or by any means, electronic or otherwise, without the prior written consent of the publisher is an infringement of copyright law

www.badatwork.com

ISBN - 1973836378

Cover Design by Kirk Thomas
Interior Image Art by Julian Gaines

Printed in the United States of America

The Making of Me

Fire, smoke, a man running past me with a TV set in a box—these were some of my earliest memories from the day I stood in the school playground with my fingers wrapped through the chain-link fence. Miramonte Elementary School was only three blocks away from the intersection of Florence Avenue and Compton, where the Watts riots were going down, right in front of me. I had been waiting for my mom to pick me up from the afterschool daycare when she got off work. I calmly watched the mayhem, heard the screaming, sirens and gunshots. I just took it all in as a sixth grader with no way of making sense of what I was seeing. A few other kids stood behind me at a safer distance, just in awe I guess or maybe too scared to run away from the scene. I heard my mom's car come screeching around the corner; I had never seen her moving so fast. She ran into the daycare, came out the side door with my younger sisters, grabbed me by the arm and yelled, "Hurry up and get in the car!" We made it home safely, but we had to take a lot of detours. When we got home, my mom immediately turned on our little black and white TV and we watched the news—the rioting was going on all over our 'hood.

As a young African American girl growing up in South Central LA, I watched the birth of the gang, the Crips, following the Watts riots as the economic decline in our community continued. Some of my older male friends talked about how joining the Crips was better than joining the Boy Scouts. At some point during this time, the late 1960's and early 1970's, I became determined to "get out and get over"—that is, to overcome my background and become successful.

My family teased me that I was "Ms. Unemotional" or "Ms. Peacemaker." I was the oldest, my mom was single off and on, and I felt like her partner. I had a lot of responsibility for helping with my siblings, cleaning the house and cooking. I had to come home right after school to babysit while my mom went to work the "swing shift"—three to eleven o'clock at night—I couldn't participate in any extracurricular activities so I read a lot. Books became my salvation. My family teased me about being a book nerd, too. By the time I got to high school, we had moved to La Puente, a lower middleclass suburb of LA. I was finally able to join the school drill team and became lieutenant, leading a squad of girls. I realized my ability to detach was a survival technique—my gift—and nothing to be ashamed of. I discovered I read people and situations really well. I had intuition about relationships. I was analytical and open to seeing things objectively. And I was good at marching drills!

Education was my ticket out of the 'hood. I went to Mt. San Antonio junior college, switched majors a few times, earned my AA degree, went on to earn a degree in psychology at the University of Oregon (Go Ducks!) and then an MBA in marketing at USC. This was at a time when women and especially women of color weren't hitting it like that. As the first person in my family to finish college, I felt had a lot to prove, mostly to myself.

I worked and traveled globally in big corporations, moving up the ladder, moving out and getting over. I've worked in consumer products—from coffee beans and food to household products. As an independent consultant, I advised service companies, nonprofits, government agencies, and academic institutions.

Learning to adapt was the biggest skill I mastered. I found that the best way to survive in corporate America was to use my childhood gifts. I watched, listened adapted and learned to be in it but not of it. I stood at the chain-link fence looking into office environments where people were "rioting"—acting badly at work. I've learned that bad behavior and bad decision-making are equal opportunity afflictions: all races, ages, genders, and organizations are susceptible.

I left corporate life and became an independent consultant in 1999 because I was frustrated with the all the interpersonal and cross-functional dysfunction that was going on. I tried to convince the leaders at the top that someone needed to pay attention and address all the poor communication and bad behavior that was going on in the rank and file. No one listened to me—they looked at me like I was an alien. So my gift of insight was not appreciated. But that rejection by Corporate America taught me to climb over the chain-link fence where I could be an objective catalyst—as an independent consultant. As an outsider, I found it was easier to see the issues in other organizations and offer my help. I had found the role that let me do my best work of analyzing, intuiting, and suggesting better ways to get work done through both people and processes.

Now years later, I still hear about the same dysfunctional behavior going on with people at work. Young people coming into the workforce today are going through the same "people issues" that I did when I was in the workplace. I see the continued dysfunction in organizations in my consulting practice. I hear about it from my colleagues. I watch my two grown children and my Millennial friends struggle to grapple with it all.

The Rundown

This is not a feel-good book. It's raw and it's real. I'm sharing my years of observing dysfunctional workplaces in the hope that I'm helping future generations find a way to play the game differently. For those of you who have only had positive experiences at work, you may think I am a Debbie Downer or just a cynic. I am telling you about the negative side of the workplace that I have actually seen and heard; nothing here is made up. This is an opportunity for you to open your eyes and ears to the reality of the madness that exists in some work environments. I am also sharing some positive stories and giving you guidelines to be a good player.

The stories here are meant to spotlight how crazy and irrational people can be at work. Maybe you'll realize that you're not alone in your experiences at work. Maybe you will think I am talking about you…and maybe I am. Maybe you'll just get a laugh. However you experience this book, that is what it is meant to be for you. If nothing else, I hope you may just figure out how to survive in this wacky world of work.

Millennials are known as "the job-hopping generation" because they change jobs more than three times the number of other workers, according to a Gallup report. It may be that these job-hoppers are looking for better opportunity. I'll buy that. But I also know for a fact that they have a very low tolerance and will leave when the people they work with and for are pricks. My generation just tolerated all the workplace crap and felt we had to stay so our resumes wouldn't reflect lack of commitment. Millennials are not motivated this way. So I'm here to tell you young people that the bad work shit you may be running from is likely to show up again in the next workplace you go to. If there is more than one person in the workplace, there is the possibility of some craziness. You've got to learn to deal with it. I'm here to help you walk through the minefields, wherever you go.

There are many books out there about all the good things that happen in the corporate world—strategies and successful product launches—but very few speak about the reality of what truly happens day-to-day, working with people. I am blessed to have a wide network of colleagues and friends who have added their stories to mine—and now I'm sharing them with you. This book is meant to help the next generation of workers and leaders to avoid making the same mistakes. What you think about the culture of a workplace before you start rarely matches the reality of working there. You need the tools to diagnose, perform triage and navigate through the sometimes-frustrating work environment.

So why is this book relevant? Because many of you experience this workplace foolishness and no one has truly spoken out about it. Because you've had a bad day at work and need to know that you're not the only person this has happened to. I want you to be aware that these things happen so you will not be surprised or blindsided. I want to you to find sanity—a mental advantage in the game. You have to work with people, and people will play games.

Each individual has to take responsibility for his or her own work life. You have options. You can step up directly to the individual who is a problem, you can ignore him, you can avoid him, you can go to your manager and complain about him, you can go up a level, you can go to HR, you can leave the company. Consider the notes after the stories—"Codas"—as lessons learned.

It's no wonder that social media and websites where you can get the inside scoop on companies with employee reviews abound. People want to say how bad things are with the company, with their manager—things that you have no one to talk to about inside the company, or may only divulge when you leave, during the exit interview. People at work need a safe place to share their feelings about what is good and bad in the workplace—to warn unsuspecting candidates of the evil that lurks within and to share the good points about the work culture of the company.

With the guidance of this book and your personal commitment, together we can stand up to the dysfunctional games played in the workplace and make the environment better for everybody.

Book Surfing

You can dip in and out of this book and find what resonates with you. The contents may seem like a random collection of thoughts and my wisdom—sort of messy, like life and life work. Just go with your own flow. Note that I am using the male pronouns generically throughout the book for ease of writing but everything pertains to both men and women. Here is a preview of the main sections, to get you started.

Part 1: Survival Guide to Keep You Alive at Work

If you've ever played a video game and reached a level you couldn't pass, a Cheat Code could help you get past it. Even if you've never played a video game, you can appreciate how shortcuts, workarounds, warnings, and advice can make life easier. That's what I'm offering you here. You'll find some of my observations and favorite principles that are most useful in dealing with people at work. My own real-life stories are peppered in to spotlight the message.

Gaming Strategies: In this section you can jump right to some Cheat Codes offering tips for dealing with some of the office games and bad players. You may still need to go back and read about the games and players to understand what you're dealing with.

Part 2: Real-Life Stories: Games People Play

You'll find stories of madness, sadness, and hilarious workplace situations. You'll find a little Coda to help you digest the learning moment–the takeaway from the situation. The stories are real, but all of the names and situations have been changed to protect the innocent and the not-so-innocent. Some stories are my own: situations I experienced first-hand in corporate life and as a consultant. Most of the stories came from colleagues who were generous in sharing them with me so I could share them with you. I have no desire to "out" anyone for acting bad at work. What you read here is intended for the good. The stories are teaching moments.

Step Up to the Plate—Be a Good Lifetime Player

This section will give you what amounts to an advanced degree on how to thrive in corporate America. I want you to be ready for the big leagues, to be that professional player who teammates and fans like because you're a good human being as well as a top scorer. You've got to pay attention to what I'm saying; you have to be willing to find other people who will share their stories with you so you can learn to survive at work. It's almost impossible bring your whole self to work safely unless you own the company and have endless money and can feel safe with failure. Otherwise you may end up in prison or in the corner with a drool cup. It's sad what happens to people in the workplace.

Part 1: Survival Guide to Keep You Alive at Work
The Culture
    Name the Game 2
    The Office Games 6
    Work Utopia 18
    This Place Sucks 21
    Workplace Culture 26
    The Vision/Mission/Values (VMV) 32
    Onboarding 34

The Boss
    A Good Leader 40
    Bad Managers & Leaders 44
    Micromanagers 47
    Tyrant/Bully Boss 50
    Cowardly Leaders 53
    Boss Child 57
    Management vs. Leadership 63

Co-Workers
    Bad Players/Sad Players 66
    Good Players—Who Do You Trust? 73
    Playground Bullies at Work 75
    Microaggressions 79
    Women at Work 81
    Not Accountable—Who Me? What? 85

Communications
    Catching Signals 89
    Game Codes 95
    Squad Goals 100
    Corporate Speak 103
    Busted Messages 108
    E-mail Can Be Evil 111
    Work Texts 114

Organizational Maneuvers
    Meeting Affective Disorder 118
    Offsite Retreats 122
    The Reorg 128

Super Powers—The Biggest Cheat Codes You'll Need
    Personal Power 134
    The Gift of Feedback 137
    Adaptability 143
    Managing Conflict 146
    Integrity 149
    Trustworthiness 151
    Manage Your Boss 155
    Office Gaming Strategies 158

Step Up to the Plate—Be a Good Lifetime Player 167
Part 2: Real-Life Stories: Games People Play 173
Resources 208

The Culture

NAME THE GAME

When I got my first "career job," the entry-level path of the corporate ladder, I was pretty naïve about the work world. I had an MBA, I had worked since I was sixteen years old, but I have never worked in a big corporation. I was lucky to get a window office in a duplex suite—meaning I had an office mate whose office was on the hallway side so I had to walk through his office to get to mine. I don't remember if I had a door, but it didn't matter because my office mate and I got along great, even though he went to Stanford and I went to rival USC. This was before the days that offices became known as cubicle farms. We had good digs. In graduate school, I learned a lot of marketing theory and business principles but I had no idea that there were other games to be played to be successful. The game in the marketing department was to impress the brand manager and the associates (next level up) with brilliant analysis, show that you could write in a disciplined, concise manner and come up with solid ideas to promote the brand and grow the business. The more covert game was to compete with the other entry-level brand assistants in your class to get promoted fast. It was an unstated competition. About twelve of us started in my class and the race was on to see who would get to go to sales training first, which was usually an indicator of who would make it to brand manager first. I quickly had to learn how to play all the games if I wanted to succeed. So, I studied the games and I became good at them. At the time, I wouldn't have called it a game, but in hindsight, that's exactly what it was.

So, I want you to have a head start in realizing that work is a game. Accept this fact and you'll be ahead of the naïve workers around you who think you just come in and do your job and that's it. I know that a game is something you play, usually a competitive activity like volleyball or Scrabble. There are winners and losers. Work is like that, too. I want you to accept the game and I want you have game. When you got game you are really good at working the situation and the politics to your advantage. You take on the challenge and say, "bring it on!" because you know the strategies and tactics you need to use. I want you to be a good work gamer. If you have the skill and ability to play the game in the office, then you got game and you will be a good player at work.

First, you have to define the game or games, being played. The company is paying you for eight-plus hours a day to do play their game—what they want, how they want it, and when they want it. They own you for that period of time, so you need to figure out if you are willing to play and if so, how you're going to play. Whoever denies this truth, whoever refuses to play, gets left on the sidelines.

Many companies are very team oriented. They encourage good working relationships and thrive because of teamwork. But don't get it twisted—some workplaces claim to be team oriented, they may not be functioning truly as a team. So don't buy into the rhetoric. If it's every man/woman for himself/herself, it's not a team game. It's ok to not be a team as long as that's clearly the game and the expectation. Maybe the games at work are not sports related. There are many professions and organizations that operate outside the team model.

When I was head of the food department at the Starbucks corporate office, I felt we were playing soccer—kicking food and beverage product concepts back and forth between departments, hoping to score a win by getting a new product all the way to the retail store, to the baristas to serve to customers. Sometimes a beverage would win;

sometimes a food item would win.

If your workplace game is sports related, here are some questions to help you name the sport at work:

- What is "the game"—the sport at your workplace?
- Is it a team sport (e.g. soccer, football, basketball)? Does it require two or more players working to get things done?
- Do you need to interact with someone else at work to get your job done or is it an individual sport (e.g. gymnastics, running, sumo wrestling)?
- Are there just two people required to play (e.g. doubles tennis, couples figure skating)?
- Who are you competing with? Are teams internally competing against each other? Are individuals competing for positions or points?
- What are the rules of the game?
- Who is the team captain?
- Who is the coach?
- Who is keeping score, giving out points, taking away points?
- Who is the referee/empire/judge?

If your workplace game is not a sports competition, here are some more questions to consider:

- Are we playing video games? Are we playing together or alone? Do I need the Cheat Codes? Are we playing online against strangers or friends?
- Are you playing fantasy football?
- Is the game played on a tabletop with counters or pieces moved and placed in pre-marked spaces?
- Is it a card game we're playing—poker, blackjack, rummy, or bid whist?
- Are we playing "Tic-tac-toe"—X's and O's?
- Is it a complex game with a lot of rules that take time to master?
- Is it a game with simple rules like checkers or chess that requires strategic thinking?
- Are we playing Monopoly, Clue, Scrabble, Dungeons & Dragons?

You've got to define the "overall game" and realize that the game changes daily as do the rules and the players. Typically, no one will tell you the game upfront. If you don't figure out the game, you may have a frustrating experience.

THE OFFICE GAMES

The Office Games are somewhat analogous to The Hunger Games book series. It's interesting to me that the author, Suzanne Collins, found some of her inspiration for the trilogy from reality TV, which is supposed to be based on unscripted real-life situations. The Office Games are also like reality TV, but the bad games are real and the plotlines can contain just as much drama and absurdity as reality TV. Fortunately, The Office Games aren't as contrived, controlled, or as brutal as The Hunger Games and there's no actual killing of children involved, thankfully.

In my first job out of graduate school, one of the bad office games was "Bed Check." We were expected to work long past normal work hours into the night and periodically, the CEO would actually come down from the twenty-fourth floor penthouse to the fifteen floor to see which of us "brand people" was really dedicated. We didn't have e-mail or Internet then so it was hard for us to warn each other when Mr. Man was on the floor after six o'clock. I played the game. I kept my fuzzy pink slippers under my desk and kicked off my sensible heels after five o'clock because I worked late most nights. I wanted to get a high score early on for dedication in the office games. I knew that the early reputation scorecard could make me or break me on the road to getting promoted.

I've worked in some great places. But no matter how great the work environment you're in, some days can be challenging. Bad stuff can happen to good people. Smart, hard-working souls can end up feeling beat down. Arrogant bastards often seem to have a fast-track ticket straight to the top.

But why does it go on in the first place?

Because business is all about competition—winning and losing. Some of it is subtle and unspoken, but nearly everyone is competing for budgets, opportunities to work on more exciting projects, customers, or resources. And then there's competition for raises, promotions, power, time with upper management, and recognition. The very fact that people do plot and scheme at work proves that politicking works and that it delivers results.

Fact: Office politics matter. You can't succeed at work without getting political. You need to learn the right buttons to push and how to influence the game-makers at work. Politics are not automatically bad and playing the political game doesn't necessarily mean you are selfish. You need to use your understanding of politics to influence people and achieve goals that are good for the organization as well as yourself. Even in the most friendly and supportive organizations, understanding office politics and how to exert influence can help you achieve outcomes that are in your best interests and the organization's best interests.

First of all, you have to choose whether you want to be a Player or a Non-Player.

Player: He undersands the importance of the unofficial rules of office politics. He knows that decisions are rarely fair or right and that decision makers have both personal as well as professional buttons that need to be pressed. The player has the gaming tools in his toolbox and uses his connections and influence to help him in the political games.

Non-Player: He focuses on his job and works hard in the hopes of being noticed and rewarded. He follows the rules and feels frustrated when decisions are not fair or right. And because he refuses to play politics, he may get taken advantage of. He ends up moaning about the unfairness at work but never doing anything about it. If you think you can succeed at work without getting political, you're wrong.

The politics are real whether you like it or not. Play the game. Or get left behind. Which are you going to do?

At work, there can be many games being played simultaneously. These games define the culture and the subcultures. Here are a few examples, in alphabetical order.

Blame Game: This game is played at all levels. The blamer will shift blame to anyone, including his dog, Duke, and anything, including the weather. He lacks the courage to stand up for his team or his mistakes, even when he knows the consequences will not affect his position. He only takes responsibility when things go right. He will not have your back. He will point the finger at you or others. The finger of the blamer just won't bend back towards himself; there's some magnetic force working against it. A cowardly boss who does not take responsibility for his action is a master of the blame game. The blamer should wear a T-shirt that says, "It's not my fault. Ever."

Chess: All of a sudden your boss wants to look good for the president of the company. He uses you as a pawn in his game to do a dog and pony show like you're a trained monkey. Don't get it twisted—your boss is all in for himself. He's not trying to spotlight you as his star employee.

Clock-Watchers: In some work places, you get points for being in your chair before start time and for staying late. It's a point system that some managers value more than is necessary, without realizing how demeaning this approach can be to compctent, capable adults. Don't even think about teleworking; you will definitely lose points. Taking paid time off (PTO) and sick days will also count against you. The clock-watcher will totally judge you. Figure out who he is and how to play to the clock game.

Cut-Down: These players are pathetic losers who can only feel good about themselves by making someone else feel stupid or inept. They specialize in sarcasm and criticism, making biting remarks that are demeaning and sometimes hurtful. It's a spin-off of the supremacy game.

Dick-swinging Contest: Despite the name, both men and women play this game. They walk around with swagger, arrogance, and superiority—like they own the place. They have to be right and have a hard time being wrong. If you try to challenge them, they will say, "Oh you have a problem with this idea? Three other people have already signed off, so deal with it."

Duck & Cover: When the shit hits the fan, a terrorist boss is on the rampage or other bad situations at work, this is the best method of personal protection. Techniques for this game: (a) hide, (b) pretend to be on your phone, (c) focus on your computer, head down, (d) take a break, or (e) go home sick.

Game of Thrones: There is a pecking order, or chain of command in the organization that must be respected. Those who dare skip over a level to try to get something done will incur the wrath of the rank they offend in the process. In the workplace, you need to stay in your lane and follow the process or you will get slapped back down to your rightful rank.

Picking Favorites: The boss makes it clear who they like the best in your workplace. The Favorite gets all the shine. He walks on water, at least for the time being. If you are in this game, you need to stay on the good side of the Favorite. If you are the Favorite, you need to watch your back because the jealous haters are going to come after you. Managers who show favoritism cause workplace conflict.

Hurry Up and Wait: You have a tough deadline to make. Your boss is breathing down your neck to get it done. You pull extra hours and deliver on time. And then, nothing happens. You ask about the next steps. Nothing. Folks are waiting on another piece or the project is no longer a priority or it's been put on hold. You feel like you busted your ass for nothing. I suggest you take a PTO day for a mental health break.

Idea Harassment: You give your boss a big idea. He agrees it's an awesome idea. As days go by and others hear about it, the idea gets watered down. The more people that get involved, the more the idea gets deflated, morphing into a dragon with no fire. It's not that these folks don't trust you or your original idea; it's actually that they all want to put their goodness into it. So guard your ideas until you have a safe harbor. This can include a support group or a champion boss to help you hold on to your truth and the right timing.

Issue Overkill – Instead of directly dealing with a person on the team who does something wrong, the manager places the issue on the agenda of the next team meeting as "policy review for X program." Most of the team knows good and well who broke the policy and will resent having to sit through the discussion. The wimpy boss is clearly avoiding handling the issue directly with the offender. This is also known as carpet-bombing.

Kissin' Ass: These players are always focused on pleasing the powerful. They shower managers with compliments, frequently request their guidance, and never openly disagree with them. Advanced players actively seek out opportunities to stroke the egos of important executives. A smart workplace bully will play this game with the boss so that when a victim comes to complain, the boss is the bully's ally. You have to know whose ass needs kissing, how to kiss it, and when. And you have to play like you're not really doing it or else you'll just be considered a loser. Also known as brown nosing—not a game for everyone, but it's real and it's an effective way to get ahead in many organizations, sadly.

Meeting Games: Some meetings are bad games. You have to: stay awake, look engaged, ask questions, and participate like you care. If you fall asleep, get caught daydreaming or texting, you will lose big points with the meeting leader and maybe others. If you are antagonistic, sarcastic, or make the wrong joke, you will lose points. If you blow off the mandatory meeting, you will be in big trouble. It's a tough game, but you've got to figure out how to play. And watch out for the meeting pirates who show up and hijack the meeting with their own agenda. (See more in the section on Meeting Affective Disorder.)

Passive Aggression: This is a pervasive game and can include some or all of the following: (a) avoiding direct contact, (b) saying something to be nice when you really don't mean it, (c) complaining to someone else about the person instead of dealing with the person directly, (d) giving in and then complaining about it later, (e) hedging or appearing to be on the fence when you really know what you want to do, and f) doing something specifically to piss someone off, but with the cover of "I didn't realize it would bother you." Some organizations have a more direct style of communication, some don't. This behavior varies by region—I've seen much more of this on the West Coast and Midwest than on the East Coast. Folks on the East Coast are much more direct—straight shooters, as they say. And there is a big variation internationally—sometimes this is the best way to play in other cultures.

Poker: In this game, you have to know when to bluff—to make a bet when you don't have all the cards in your hand. Only do this when you have a high degree of confidence in what you're presenting at work. Make it sound good and the powers that be may bite. You also need to know when to keep a poker face—don't let them see you sweat and don't say anything. As we've heard Kenny Rogers tell us, holding 'em and folding 'em are both great options. So is walking away, and running isn't bad, either!

Pretend: If you choose to play this game because you can't leave the job right now, protect your soul. Wear the necessary mask at work and play the part that goes with it; don't get too into character. Check your real self at the door only temporarily, like an actor on screen or in a play. Read today's work script, and understand your motivation for each scene. Step into the role, play it well, then go home and be your real self. Hopefully, you only have to play this game temporarily for a short time until you find your next gig.

Reviver: Everyone wants to say they contributed to the success of a product that was dying and has now been resuscitated. When the product was dying, no one wanted to be near it. They all wanted to focus on something else. Now that your team and you have found ways to make the product relevant again, everyone says they knew it wasn't dead.

Scapegoating: In this game, somebody is quickly identified as the cause of the problem—guilty without a trial. Scapegoating can resemble a tennis match, with blame-shifting conversation going back and forth. This game can be played not just with an individual, but also with entire departments—Team Scapegoat. Scapegoating detracts from the real issue, so the problem doesn't get rectified, but the guilty party instead gets skewered. If the boss is a chronic player, the game can be career threatening for the little Billy goat.

Sink or Swim: You have a new assignment. No one to train you, no instructions, no written history of how it was done in the past. They throw you into the deep and assume you know how to swim. You realize that no one is going to help you out; you've got nowhere to turn for help. It's all on you. You've got to put on your big boy or big girl pants and take care of yourself. Period. You might think someone would have your back—your manager, your peers, maybe even HR. Good luck figuring it out.

Snubbing: This is a team game that requires a victim—someone to punish for being different. Gradually the victim realizes that he is being excluded from the group. Because it is a childish game, the players are immature and small-minded. If the target ever gets promoted over these players who messed with him, watch out.

Sorority/Fraternity: The power cliques run the place. It could be a department—Sales is more important than Marketing or Real Estate is more important than Product Development—or just a group of random folks. The players here are not necessarily hostile, they just enjoy being part of their special little clique. Communication with them may be pleasant, but everyone knows that an invisible barrier exists. It's similar to snubbing, but more passive aggressive. It's not about punishment, it's simply that you are either in or you are out—it's a power play. This game is really unfair when the frat boys/sorority girls make business decisions that involve you, without you. Ha, ha!

Squawking: Instead of taking the time to get his facts straight, this leader bursts into a project, squawking up a storm, criticizing, proposing changes then takes off leaving little piles of shit steaming on the table for everyone else to clean up.

Suggestion Jerk-Off: Management says they want suggestions from employees, but they really don't mean it. People submit their ideas for improvements or new products/services and nothing ever happens. Or even worse, your manager steals your idea and you get no credit. Note to managers: Unless you have a process to realistically assess ideas and an intention to move forward with implementation of ideas, then don't ask. It's very unfulfilling for the idea submitters who thought they were at least going to have sex with someone, not just themselves.

Supremacy: A player in this game actually believes he is more important than anyone else and untouchable. When his real life isn't impressive enough, a dedicated player will actually make up some ridiculousness about himself. Supremacy usually has only one player, someone who is simply in search of an audience. But when two players compete, the game becomes "Mine's bigger than yours"—even with the women.

Survival of the Fittest: The best game players live to see the next day, to get raises, and to get promoted. It's not just about being the smartest or the most physically energetic. Those that survive in the work world have the whole package—political savvy as well as the skills and talents to do the job. Unless the way to survive is Kissin' Ass, then the skills needed to survive are different. You need to figure out how to survive and thrive at work, because Darwin's theory has new meaning in the workplace.

Visibility: As long as you have something that's visible enough for everyone to see, you're in. Smart move is to only spend time on things that get you noticed. If you think you can just do your job and be a good employee, you will become invisible. The promotion gods will not even know your name. You are your own best marketer of your brand. Period. That is, until you get a champion to be your promoter.

War Games: Too often at work, competition is set up for internal battles between individuals and/or between departments. This is when it gets really political at work. You may be tempted to take on every battle. Most battles really aren't worth fighting at work. Save your energy for the ones that really matter, that you have passion for and hopefully, an advocate to watch your back when you approach the enemy. Otherwise, let the little stuff go. It's just not worth the fight. (See more in the section on Managing Conflict)

These games are played within the overall game. You've got to learn to recognize the specific game in the moment and change your game plan accordingly.

Most work games are based on ego—the desire for power, the need to control others, the need to bolster self-worth/ego or the need to divert attention or procrastinate. Most of the games are founded in people's insecurities, low self-esteem, and inadequacies.

Ego Games: The player needs to feel smarter, better, or more special than other people. It's all about ego. Some games require a victim, while others just allow the players to puff themselves up a bit. Most of these game players are actually masking strong feelings of insecurity or inferiority.

Control/Power Games: The player is trying to either increase his leverage or flaunt his existing power by controlling others. Some players have malicious intentions, while others are merely self-centered. All power games are designed to give the player some type of advantage over other people.

Diversion/Avoidance Games: The purpose of a diversion game is to avoid unpleasant consequences. The player is a) trying to avoid blame, b) passively dodge responsibility, c) afraid to confront an issue, or d) hoping to be invisible.

Political maneuvering is just part of office life and games have a specific purpose. Political games are always played for emotional rewards. The player will resist any attempt to change the game, because he doesn't want to lose the emotional payoff. The player will often try to give logical explanations for everything he does without ever stating his true motives.

People are emotional beings with conflicting wants, needs, biases, and insecurities. If your antennas are up, you'll see that the bad player's actions will start to form a predictable pattern. More people than you might think are lying to get ahead, gossiping, and bitching about their frustrations. Put all of this together and you've got a highly politically charged work environment.

CHEAT CODES:

If you want to do more than just survive at work, you have to play, but you don't have to play dirty.

You need to sharpen your game skills.

Your best strategy is to be grounded by self-awareness and self-management.

You can't change the player, but you can choose how you want to play. Your game plan doesn't have to descend into lying, cheating, and backstabbing.

Treat politics like the game it is, but don't let it into your soul.

Questions to Consider:
- Based on the list of office games, can you identify which ones are power games, which are ego games, and which are escape games?
- What other games can you identify at work?
- Can you think of strategies for dealing with those games?

WORK UTOPIA

People want to be able to enjoy the place where they spend most of their waking hours. You can find amazing places to work driven by great leaders who understand the importance of focusing on their people. Here are just some of the important characteristics of a place where I would want to work, where The Good Office Games are played and there is A Good Culture.

Creativity Welcomed Here: Your ideas are encouraged, nurtured and given life. Even if one of your suggestions doesn't make the cut, you still feel heard and respected. And you will bring more ideas even after some rejection.

Culture of Collaboration: Everyone actually knows how to keep their ego in balance so they are able to be vulnerable, be open, and therefore able to create new approaches.

Gold Stars: You are recognized for your contributions, no matter how small. You get kudos not just at your annual review but whenever you do something well. Everyone celebrates each other's successes.

Honest Leadership: Leaders are open, approachable, honest and direct. They keep politics to a minimum. They are fair, objective and encourage pushback and critique of themselves.

Living the VMV: The vision, mission, and values are alive and well, not just words on a poster. People walk the talk and keep focus on what's important. Everyone is on the same page.

Minimal Politics: Politics are always going to happen in any work environment, but good organizations work to stomp it out when it slinks in.

Open Book: Everyone can bring their whole selves to work without fear. You can ask questions, challenge one another and the status quo, play devil's advocate, and speak openly.

Passionate Players: The people who work here are not just here for a paycheck. They truly care about the work, want to make things better and are willing to help one another.

Play Hard, Work Hard: It's a fun place to work where everyone works hard but keeps a good balance of humor. The work environment is conducive to creativity—interesting seating arrangements, comfortable places to meet or have private time, inspiring ambiance (art on the walls, temperature controls, real sunlight, etc.).

Teamwork is Real: I've got your back and you've got mine. Everyone works well together. If you are falling behind, one of your teammates will step up to help you. The leader lifts everyone up to be the best they can be. We're all in it to win it together.

This Place Rocks: You love working here. You enjoy your colleagues, you're passionate about your work, you believe in the organization, leadership is great, you enjoy going in each day and you don't mind working extra hours.

I worked for a company that really rocked. If you are lucky, you will get one of these experiences in a lifetime—most people never do. We were a true team. If anyone on the management team was struggling, we were all there to help, even it meant coming in on a weekend to help the warehouse with inventory. We pulled together when our parent company decided to sell our division—we put a proposal together to do an initial public offering to give the parent the price they wanted so we could stay together as an intact management team and not risk being broken up by an outside buyer. Fortunately, we pulled it off and went from being a division of Weyerhaeuser to a new company—Paragon Trade Brands. One of the proudest moments in my career!

I'm hoping you can add to this list of good workplace experiences. It would warm my heart.

Questions to Consider:

- What makes a good workplace—an environment you really enjoy going there five days a week, fifty weeks of the year?
- What do you produce that makes you feel good at work—the equivalent of watching your garden grow?

THIS PLACE SUCKS

You know your job sucks when the highlight of your day would be to get laid off. Here's what you'll see in a workplace that bites:

- Bad-mouthing the company
- Intimidation
- Disinterest
- Overly controlling management
- No appreciation for hard work
- Poor decision making
- Manipulation
- Carelessness
- Not accepting responsibility
- Apathy
- Just doing the minimum required
- Not enough resources (people, equipment, budget, capital)
- No trust
- No fun

When you spend most of your daily life in a toxic environment, you will get physically sick—stomachaches, headaches, shortness of breath and feeling extremely stressed out. No one should ever have to work in this kind of environment, but it's pretty normal, in reality. I know sometimes you have to tolerate it until you can find a safe haven. It's important to listen to your intuition. You may become immune to a bad workplace and convince yourself that it's worse to leave. I hate to see fear keep you from moving on to a better place, but I know it happens. You'll know when you've had enough, hopefully before you become too bitter and cynical. Then you may need to move on to another organization. Or you can do I did—go start your own business. Know this, you may save your soul but you will lose the comfort of a regular paycheck.

I saw a lot of dysfunction when I was at one place where I worked. The departments competed with each other and didn't talk to each other. Everyone was pursuing their own agenda—pulling power plays and engaging in political maneuvers. I wanted to help so I put together a proposal to become the person that helped glue the functions together—an internal consultant, like an organizational development professional, which didn't exist at the time. I took my proposal to HR—in hindsight, that was the wrong place to go—and the director looked at me like I had two heads. HR couldn't understand what I was talking about—they really had no clue about what was going on with the business units. HR suggested I just leave the company and start my own consulting practice. I didn't really want to leave the company. A few weeks later, my manager called me in and gave me a severance package. It turned out to be a win/win because I got money to leave and start my own business, which turned out to be the best decision of my life.

Some work environments are downright hostile, as defined legally. When a boss or coworker's behavior is discriminatory and makes doing your job impossible, that's hostile. A coworker who tells sexually explicit jokes, sends dick pics, and recommends obnoxious porn sites is guilty of sexual harassment. Again, that is legally creating a hostile work environment. A boss who gets on your case about your gender, religion, race, or age may be guilty, as well. Even if these comments are played as jokes, the boss may be creating a hostile work environment. If you have asked individuals to stop and they don't, then there could be a lawsuit in the making.

You'll know that it's time to leave when:

- You begin to question your own worth and start losing confidence in your abilities.
- You aren't heard—no one is listening to what you have to say.
- You work for a boss who encourages bad behavior and stirs up too much competitive conflict.

- Your boundaries aren't being respected—your time, your values.
- You don't feel like getting up and going into the place, at all.
- Your personal life is pathetic—work-life balance is totally out of whack.
- Your friends and family notice a difference in your spirit.
- You are constantly getting sick.
- You are really unhappy.
- Your boss is blocking you from growing, taking credit for your work, or giving you assignments way beneath your skill level.
- Your boss is unethical.
- Your co-workers are complete knuckleheads.

Realize this: none of this is a reflection on you or who you are. The environment that surrounds you daily can really start to affect your self-worth. You've got to learn to separate the negativity you are dancing around daily from the reality of your being. It takes a lot of your energy to combat the foolishness day after day.

Here are some survival tips while you're stuck in a bad workplace:

CHEAT CODES:

Put some positive/uplifting quotes on your screen saver or around your cubicle walls.

Take a walk every day at lunchtime to get some fresh air, reboot and remind yourself that nature exists and you are really ok.

Put a sticky note on your desk and make a tick mark every time some bull goes down that bothers you and you don't allow it to upset you or react to it. If you do react, subtract a previous tick mark.

Accept the fact that you can't ever control other people; they are going to be who they are so don't buy into their negativity.

Find some ways to improve yourself—reading, going to lectures, taking classes/seminars or joining a book club. You need as many ways to escape the situation you're in as possible, so you might as well get some personal growth.

Learn what you can from the craziness and use it to make a good decision about your next workplace and about how you want to be as a manager and leader—not like these fools.

There are some great places to work. I hope you'll find a place that's healthy and enjoyable—a place where you'll feel valued. Even the best work environment has some craziness to deal with, so don't expect perfection. People are people and they bring their baggage with them everywhere they go. You can find a great manager who supports you, strong leadership at the top, co-workers you like and respect and a positive atmosphere.

WORKPLACE CULTURE

Culture is invisible—you can't see it or touch it, but you can feel it. It includes the physical environment but it's the intangible parts that make it real. You can walk into a cool, modern office space that looks very casual, with lots of open space, and think, "Wow, this looks like a really cool company to work for." But is it really? Just like in dating relationships, physical attractiveness can be deceiving. You like what you see, you get a vibe and you go with it. Then after a few dates, the devil or witch or some other scary character appears. Damn! What happened?

At work, it's the same way. What really determines the true mood or tone of the workplace is the leadership style, the people who work there, and the organizational structure and processes. You will not often find a written document that describes the culture and yet it is one of the most important elements of the employee experience. Business magazine sites rank what they describe as "companies with great workplace culture"—so you can at least get a sense of these workplaces. But what about the thousands of companies that don't make these lists? Either the corporate culture will energize, motivate and empower you or it will suffocate, drain and discourage you. Maybe on a given day it varies but you're hoping for the more positive cultural experience on a day-to-day basis.

There is often a big gap between what the organization claims to be and what it is really like on a day-to-day basis. Some organizations talk a good game—on their websites and in their press releases—but don't deliver. There are good and bad work cultures.

Here are some elements that cumulatively define an organization:

- Leadership
- How people behave
- Who gets hired
- Who gets promoted
- The real values vs. the stated values
- The practices and processes—how the work gets done
- What and who gets rewarded
- The dress code
- The informal rules

Every organization has a distinct culture; leadership sets the tone for the personality, behaviors, and standards. Some cultures are very hands on; others are very analytical. Some workplace cultures are fun and playful, others are very cold and serious. It's more of a concept. You can't see culture with your eyes, but you can feel the invisible force at work—how people behave, who gets hired, the relationships between departments, how customers are treated, who gets promoted and rewarded. Like turning a huge fleet of ships, it's hard to change the culture. It's alive, breathing, and won't adapt easily.

You can Google an organization, go to the "About Us" page and read their stated Vision/Mission/Values and maybe even a description of their culture, but know that these are just words—the desired state of affairs. You can also go to social media and third-party websites and read employee reviews, the pros and the cons, of working for the company, but it's still a crapshoot.

For every company culture, there are upsides and downsides, even for the ones on the Best Companies to Work For lists. Every culture is unique but I like these broad categories (by no means a definitive list), with some of the pluses and minuses for each.

Start-Up Corporate Culture
Hierarchy is irrelevant, more collaboration

UPSIDES	DOWNSIDES
Everyone pitches in	Smaller team size
Have to be a "jack of all trades"	Less infrastructure
More nimble	Limited capabilities
Extraordinary customer service	Constant pressure to survive
Takes more risks	Financial instability
Very responsive to market research	Chaos
Lots of informal communication	Hard to keep talent

Team-Oriented Corporate Culture
Cultural fit is most critical factor

UPSIDES	DOWNSIDES
Employee happiness is top priority	Hard to maintain with growth
Frequent team outings	Slow/long decision making
Departments mingle	Loose infrastructure
Feedback welcomed	More meetings
Flexible work schedules	Lack of accountability

Intense Corporate Culture
Fearless desire to change the status quo

UPSIDES	DOWNSIDES
Hires highly competitive types	Intense work environment
Always pushing the envelope	Highly competitive internally
Needs employees to lead the way	Pressure to always be "on"
Innovative and daring	Pushes the envelope
Fast growth	Insecurity
Challenging is encouraged	High performance expectations
Employees make work their top priority	Long hours expected
Fast promotion track	No training

Conservative Corporate Culture
Big company, old school management style

UPSIDES	DOWNSIDES
Dress code is conservative	People stay in their silos
Numbers-focused	Not cutting edge on social media
Bottom line takes precedence	Lack flexibility in work style
Strong infrastructure	Slow to change office technology
Financial stability	Risk-averse decision making
Clear roles and responsibilities	Traditional performance review
Definite training programs	People don't socialize much

Transitioning Corporate Culture
Unsettled due to merger or new management

UPSIDES	DOWNSIDES
Change can be exciting	Expectations unknown
Great chance to shift goals and mission	Fear due to change
Fresh start	High turnover
Opportunity to try new ideas	Tension between old and new
Possibly more resources	Requires patience
More stability	Layoffs and reorganization

It's hard to get a good handle on the true culture of an organization when you're not in it. Questions to consider when interviewing with a potential employer or even to assess your current culture:

Questions to Consider:
- What type of culture do you currently work for?
- What is the ideal culture for your style?
- How does management really interact with the employees?
- How is professional growth supported?
- How is failure handled?

- What behaviors get rewarded?
- How do decisions get made?

CHEAT CODES:

Adjusting to a new workplace or even a new department in the same work environment takes time so be patient, listen a lot, and observe.

Find a mentor to help you navigate office norms. That special someone on your team who has a good understanding of how the workplace culture works and can help you avoid a misstep until you figure things out.

Get involved with folks outside of the office to network and learn.

If you're already in an organization and you're seeing discrepancies between the talk versus the walk, you need to assess if the walk fits with what you want in a work environment.

If you see a big gap between your values and the organization and you can afford to walk away, you may have to do this when the culture doesn't fit you.

You can stay and play the game, but it takes more energy and it may cost you your soul.

You can't change the direction of the wind, but you can adjust your sails on your little skiff. If the culture suits you, you are in a great situation.

When you're looking for a new job, my best advice is to ask the potential employer if you can speak with a few employees—some in the department you're being considered for, some outside. If you're lucky, you'll get some straight answers. Here are a few simple questions, in addition to the ones previously mentioned, to ask your potential colleagues:

Questions to Consider:
- What's your favorite thing about working with people here?
- What's your least favorite thing about working with people here?
- If you could wave a magic wand, what would you change about the way people interact with each other here?
- Do people have fun? How?
- Do people feel appreciated?

THE VISION/MISSION/VALUES (VMV)

The VMV statements are meant to define the desired culture and goals of the organization. If you are fortunate enough to work for an organization that does live out its vision, mission, and values on a daily basis, that is awesome and as it should be! It's one of the keys to a successful, healthy, productive, and pleasant work environment. I have worked with clients who have achieved a healthy workplace where everyone truly lives the VMV. When the VMV come to life, it's a beautiful thing!

I have facilitated some sessions with organizations to create or re-evaluate their vision, mission, and values. In these sessions, folks in the room really establish what they want to stand for, where they're going, and how they want to behave on that journey. The words are usually awesome, clear, and inspiring and get posting the words on the wall, on the website, and in the employee handbook.

What bothers me most is that some leaders who attend the VMV creation session don't live the intentions they espoused at the workshop. I really wish this wasn't true. I've checked in later with my clients and their employees and found that sometimes, some of the leaders don't walk the talk. To me, it's just a show to have the VMV statements if leadership doesn't truly live them. And then leadership wonders why the organization isn't reflective of the stated on the VMV statement.

Now to be fair, I have seen organizations with strong VMV that they genuinely live daily. When everyone in the organization uses the language in the vision, mission and values regularly—in conversation, as priority setting and decision making tools and as a way to recognize each other—then these statements have meaning. And for extra credit, when customers and other outsiders know the company's principles, that when true awesomeness exists. VMV come to life when the leadership visibly champions the statements—they walk the talk, they lead by example and make everyone proud to follow them. Great VMV statements can fire up employees to go beyond expectations and create a special place to work.

"Vision without action is merely a dream. Action without vision just passes the time. Vision with action can change the world." Joel A. Barker, author and businessman

ONBOARDING

Welcome! You've been hired. Let the honeymoon begin. Some companies make a huge investment in getting new employees introduced to the culture and socializing them to their new organization. Some don't do much of anything except have you sign up for benefits and send you to your cubicle.

Good employers know that new employees make up their minds in the first 90 days about whether to stay in their job. As a newbie, you go through the orientation and you may get to meet some of the executives. You sit in a conference room with other new hires and hear all about what a great place this is to work. It's sounds all beautiful and fluffy like Disneyland. You're all aglow, virtually holding hands with your new boss and co-workers. It's the honeymoon period. Enjoy the frequent sex upfront, because it won't last.

Onboarding is a type of socialization—an introduction to your new tribe, your new culture. It's a way to bring in new employees and get them acclimated to the organization. If the company could, they would just give you a pill or a drink and you would immediately know how to fit in—but they can't. It's kind of like joining a fraternity or sorority, but without the hazing. Usually, you sit in a room with the other newbies for a few hours or maybe as many as five days, learning about the company's history, vision, mission, values, strategies, and goals. You may get to see the org chart, a leader or two may come in to speak, maybe even join you for lunch. You hear all the really good stuff, the stuff that gets you even more pumped now that you're actually here signing all the HR paperwork, choosing your benefits and automatic payment for your check.

Onboarding should be a legitimate attempt to welcome you into your new company family. Without this process, it is really hard in those first ninety days to get your feet planted firmly on the ground and understand how things work. It's in the organization's best interest to get you off to a good start. After all, some investment was made in recruiting you, interviewing you, spending time with you and now the company needs to get a return on the initial investment they made in getting you through the door. It's time to get assimilated you into the culture, hopefully in the best way possible that is genuinely going to reflect your experience at your desk—when you leave the safety of the conference room with your new cohorts.

What some organizations call onboarding is really just another word for orientation. Orientation is generally a one-time event. Good onboarding should be a continuous process for sixty to ninety days, involving a variety of immersion activities and opportunities to learn what every function does—visiting headquarters, manufacturing and research facilities, retail or restaurant locations, and all aspects of the business. It should be more than getting the handbook and then meeting your teammates. You and your manager should meet regularly and if you could be assigned a mentor or big brother that would really speed the company bonding process along.

Many years ago when I started at a certain company, I was surprised at the lack of any orientation or onboarding process. Unfortunately, I started Christmas week, one of the most high-pressure times of the year for the company. The day I started, there was a crisis—holiday sales were way below expectation. So with this backdrop, I arrived at the corporate reception desk, gave my name and waited almost an hour before anyone came to get me. My new boss was in an emergency meeting with the CEO and all the other executives, strategizing what to do about the sluggish sales. So when my boss eventually got a free moment, she called one of my new peers and told him to come get me. I had never met the guy. He was nice enough, but it was awkward—he had no idea what to do with me. An office hadn't even been set up for me. So I sat in his cubicle and chatted. Eventually, my new boss got out of her meeting and took me to her office where we chatted for an hour. Of course, she apologized for the chaos. By the end of the day, she got me set up in a cubicle and gave me some documents to read. I think later the next day, someone from HR called me to come fill out my benefits forms. That was it. I still kept my enthusiasm for my new job because I had so much respect for the company. Lucky for them, I stayed and didn't go running out of the building in tears that first day.

The Set Up

You have a computer, a phone, a desk, and a chair. You even have a nameplate. Yippee! Now you start your work and you have questions. People say, "Didn't you read the handbook?" Now you feel neglected, underappreciated, overwhelmed. It's not fun. You're wondering, "What happened to all that good upfront sex?" Not only that, but you thought you were hired to play the drums and now they've handed you a trumpet—an instrument you have no familiarity with. It's different work than you expected. You lose your confidence.

After a few weeks, your rose-colored glasses become clearer and you see a culture of fear, passive aggression, no trust, the loudest person in the room winning, and other dysfunctional behavior. You realize it's overwhelming, it's not fun, and you're not sure it's safe. You sit on the toilet, the seat is up, and you fall in. The problem is there is no further investment in you after the onboarding phase; unless you have a manager who takes the time to extend your assimilation experience. And it seems that everyone else in the place that has been there a while didn't drink the same Kool-Aid they gave out at the onboarding session. You were thinking of buying a plant for your desk, but now you're hesitating. You ask yourself, "Will I survive this place?" You might want to hold off on that plant purchase for your desk.

Good onboarding needs to extend for at least ninety days and it involves a big time commitment on the part of the manager and the team. Everyone needs to be invested in getting the new hire off to a great start, beyond the orientation. You really need to know what is expected of you, what the learning curve is like, and have constant feedback on how you're doing. This first three months are when you can ask any questions, no matter how trivial, so you can get all the info you need to be successful upfront.

CHEAT CODES:

You've got to find a mentor, a colleague you can trust who will give you the true lowdown. Often this can be the lowest level but longest tenured person around—admin, coordinator, someone in the know.

Choose your person carefully; take them to lunch where you can speak privately.

You're on a climb of Mount Everest—on a new learning curve—and you need a Sherpa guide to show you the best route, to show you the ropes in place and to help you carry your gear, metaphorically.

If you're going to survive in this new workplace, you need a lot of help, so maybe get into a group. If there's a sports rec league or some other after work activities you enjoy, join up.

Try not to compare your job to the last one you had—it's not fair and it won't help you adjust to the new work environment. And don't talk about how much better your old job was. That's a serious mistake.

Reserve judgment.

Take notes.

Figure out who has the power.

Begin to understand the unspoken rules.

Make sure you really understand the whole situation before you start getting critical.

Be prepared to make mistakes—it's ok, you're a newbie.

Try to fit in as best you can.

Be on your best behavior, like you're on a date.

Don't start off cursing and trying to be too cool. Wait a while till you understand the way other people talk.

Be careful about your jokes—you don't know if these folks will share your sense of humor.

Make your mark as soon as you can. Prove that you were the right hire.

Don't bluff. If you don't know how to do something, ask.

The Boss

A GOOD LEADER

A good leader knows how to get the best out of his team. He knows that as long as there is more than one person in the workplace, there will be some kind of emotional drama and as the manager/leader, he will be expected to referee, counsel, chastise, coach, and resolve issues. His goal is to create an environment where people learn how to resolve their own dramas and stop coming to Papa or Mama for solutions. A good leader also knows how to manage up—to support his team with the powers that be and have influence up the chain of command.

Here are some criteria I look for in a good leader. He or she is:

Introspective—able to look critically at their own strengths, weaknesses and behavior with the goal of constantly growing and getting better.

Inspiring—passionate about the work, the people, and the outcomes in a way that goes viral.

Committed to building others up—wants everyone on the team to grow and be successful; isn't afraid to give away responsibility.

Focused—has a clear vision of where the team needs to stretch and repeats the strategy for getting there constantly with enthusiasm; keeps his eye on the long term reward.

Accountable—takes responsibility for his own actions and holds everyone else equally accountable; doesn't let people get away with bad behavior or performance.

Courageous—comfortable having straight conversations.

Emotionally stable—able to control his emotions and stay calm in the face of others' emotional breakdowns and crises.

Credible—has the goods, knowledge, insight and expertise. Deserves props.

Respected—gives followers enough swag and assertiveness to earn their respect, but isn't too arrogant.

Instinctive—has the ability to read people and situations well.

Full of Integrity—does the right thing all day, every day, with authenticity.

Open-minded—encourages trying new things and doesn't smack you down when you fail.

Patient—willing to give ideas and people a chance to thrive in a reasonable timeframe.

Transparent—keeps it real, shares all the info, doesn't pull any punches, and admits his own mistakes.

Resourceful—finds ways to get his team what they need to be successful—equipment, software, staff, or outside help.

Fair—treats each individual the same and is objective about reviewing performance.

Your boss is there to lead and manage—not to be friends with staff. He has to evaluate your performance and make decisions about getting the work done, and those responsibilities can create conflict in the friendship/relationship. You can be friends, but just don't lose sight of the end game—getting results.

One of the best leaders I worked for had five simple focus points for the entire organization. He would repeat these points at every opportunity: at staff meetings, when he went out to ride along with salespeople, when he was at the manufacturing plant or wherever he was in the company. The outcome was that you could ask anyone what those five things were and they could tell you. We were able to judge our priorities, resources, budgets and actions by whether or not those items fit the "Focus on Five." Sounds corny and boring, but it was effective. The other thing this leader did was to get in the trenches. About once a month, he would travel to one of the plants and work for an hour on the production line, shocking the hourly workers, He'd go on customer calls. He'd sit in on functional staff meetings. He wasn't a micromanager; he just wanted people to know that he cared about what everyone was doing. He touched people's heads and hearts, figuratively. Even when times were bad, we all rallied around him.

I look for a leader who sits back quietly, letting his people flourish and empowering them to grow. This leader knows when to step up, give direction, or take action. He cares little for the trappings of leadership, focusing instead on setting the example for their peers and followers. He seeks out opinions and builds relationships. He knows that mutual respect fosters trust. A good leader anticipates and acts before he needs to. A truly courageous leader makes the tough decisions and models the behaviors that foster organization and a good work environment.

Questions to Consider:

- What's your definition of a good leader?
- Bosses need to hear positive feedback too so they can keep doing the good things you like. How would you write one of these letters to your current or past boss?
- "Dear Boss, I want to thank you for the way you…."
- "Dear Boss, Last week at the ____ when you___, I really appreciated the way you handled___."
- "Dear Boss, You gave me the chance to ____ and I know you took a chance on me. I really appreciate how you ____."

BAD MANAGERS & LEADERS

Bad leaders come in all sizes, shapes and genders. The big bosses—CEO, President, Executive Director, and Vice President—often allow themselves to get so removed from the day-to-day that they have no true idea of the ability of all their players. They make some decisions in this vacuum or they rely on the sometimes, questionable advice from their direct reports, who have their own political agendas. They set the tone for the whole organization and if they're really bad, they cause lots of damage to individuals and to the culture.

Lower on the org chart, below the big bosses, are some bad managers and supervisors who typically have no business leading people—no natural ability and/or no training in leading people. A bad manager probably got promoted for all the wrong reasons—maybe because he kissed enough ass. He provides no value but gets paid good money. Why not be that guy who makes his direct reports better? He doesn't know how or he doesn't care. Instead, he drains good energy from others, underutilizes talented people, and takes away from his team's ability to produce their best results.

I worked for a boss who was really smart, but really bad as a manager and leader. He overwhelmed us with work, cracked the whip, and talked to us like we were children. I warned him that I had to leave before my car got locked in the company garage at nine o'clock and he said I couldn't leave until I finished. So I had to take a cab home around nine thirty. No dinner break, either. Next morning when I came in, there was a little gift box on my desk. When I opened it, I saw it contained a little wallet and a thank-you note from my boss. I didn't appreciate it.

No boss should ever make you feel like you're not smart enough or good enough for the position you are in, especially when you know you are doing your very best. Some bosses are just not good leaders and never will be so don't take it personally. You have to take care of yourself first. There are better bosses in the world. The remaining sections in this book will help you countermove against those bad managers and leaders.

CHEAT CODES:

Work on yourself first. Do an objective inventory of your strengths and weaknesses and how you may be contributing to the problem with your boss.

Manage your emotions. Don't counterattack. Be professional. Always.

Pick your battles carefully.

Talk to your boss and make sure you are on the same page about expectations of each other.

Listen well. Think before you speak.

Politely tell your boss exactly what you need from him.

Ask your boss how you can help him reach his goals.

Don't tell him that he's a bad boss. That won't help the situation.

Try to find something your boss is good at and focus on that. Learn from him.

Don't try to kiss up to your boss. That would be insincere.

Have regular check-ins to keep him informed. Be proactive. Don't surprise him.

MICROMANAGERS

We all have a need for a sense of control, because when we feel out of control, we get really uncomfortable. Some people have an extreme need to control people and things—these people are control freaks. They need to know everything and direct every nuance of a situation. They want to make sure they don't look bad to the folks above them. In general, they often don't trust anyone else to do things right. When you trust others, you can relinquish the need to control them. When you don't trust others, you feel the need to exert your power over them.

The control freak as a boss has an intense need to micromanage their direct reports. This type of manager has something to say about everything you do—what you say, how you act, how you dress, even what you think. You can't be yourself around them. Control freaks want to influence your work life in every way possible. They can show no respect for you or your boundaries. The micromanager needs to know every damn detail of the work his direct reports are doing. He's motivated by insecurity, lack of trust, and fear of being blamed for the mistakes of others. He is definitely a buzz kill to all of the truly competent people who work for him. He will drive the best people away from the organization.

When you are really competent and confident in your job, you don't need to be controlled or micromanaged. If you do get this control freak coming at you, you may shut down, get angry, lose productivity, or quit. It's overwhelming, disrespectful, and annoying when you know you're competent and some controlling manager tries to run your work life. It's a total mismatch—competent employee and controlling boss—and a recipe for disaster. If you're working for or with a control freak, you've got to earn their trust by building proof that you can deliver without their interference. Get in front of them before they come at you—be proactive in letting them know that you really got this, by showing them your plan of attack.

There are some people who actually like to be controlled, especially when they lack confidence or have been puppets in their lives. We should find these puppets and put them all in a building with all the control freaks where they can live happily ever after.

CHEAT CODES:

You need to be flexible and patient. Don't get aggravated when this boss is standing over your shoulder watching you work.

Always show that you know your job well; competence will eventually buy you some breathing room.

Identify the control freak's need. Try to anticipate the micromanager's need for information. Get in front of his requests, even if it feels like a waste of your time.
  - *Does he need detailed timelines? Then give him the hour-by-hour game plan.*
  - *Does he love to revise documents? Then give him rough drafts that he can redline to death.*
  - *Does he need lots of communication? Then e-mail and text him more than you normally would someone else.*

Don't let his requests make you feel bad about yourself.

Try to gain his trust by showing him you've got his back.

Let him get involved early on projects versus towards the middle or end. He'll feel better the more he knows.

Show him you know your stuff. It won't stop him, but maybe he'll back off a little.

Remember that his need to micromanage is his problem, not yours. He feels insecure and masks it with controlling behaviors.

Set some grown-up boundaries. Don't let a controlling boss treat you like a child, put you down or use you like a doormat.

Give yourself kudos for the good job you do. And give yourself extra credit for keeping a good attitude while working for a detail/control freak.

Don't let him make you feel inadequate or get you down.

If your boss has low knowledge and competence, you may have to swallow your pride and do some of his work for him.

TYRANT/BULLY BOSS

The bully boss is the most dangerous type of bully because he has position power and gets to kick some ass directly. The ordinary co-worker bully is no fun either (See more in the section on Playground Bullies at Work). In his role over others, his direct reports become the innocent workplace victims of his intentional meanness. Intimidation is the main approach of this leader. This boss will eat your flesh—picking and pecking at you little by little. He is the master of taking down the self-esteem of his team members. It is likely that the tyrant or bully boss is dealing with some unresolved anger from childhood, one way or another. On the schoolyard, maybe this kid stomped around, pushed other kids around, and made fun of them. Or maybe he was a victim of bullying himself and now he needs to get revenge on the world. Some of his bullying behaviors include:

- Yelling, cursing
- Verbal abuse, name calling
- Throwing temper tantrums
- Personal criticizing
- Intimidating you physically
- Spreading rumors about you; talking behind your back
- Extreme micromanaging
- Harshly criticizing your work
- Questioning your skills in front of others; humiliating you
- Setting you up for failure by giving you outrageous deadlines or constantly changing the parameters of your assignment
- Blaming you for things beyond your control
- Blocking your attempts to get transferred or promoted

- Making it clear you are not his favorite
- Keeping you out of the limelight
- Denigrating your opinion
- Demeaning you
- Dissing you
- Taking credit for your work
- Calling/texting you at all hours of the night and weekend

In certain workplace cultures, this character can get away the bully behavior. The folks upstairs don't see it, don't care to see it, or actually are ok with his bad behavior because the tyrant boss is a smart, productive guy. It's easy for upper management to turn their heads at his abuse when he's delivering the profit. If this person is rewarded with promotion for his technical skills and results, he will continue to perpetuate the climate of fear. The bully then gets reinforcement and thinks, "Well they need me and I'm bulletproof. No one is going to touch me. I can do anything I want." In a work culture that values results over people, tyrants and bullies thrive as leaders, sad to say.

Bullies see themselves as better than others, which justifies their bad behavior. They generally have no sensitivity to others' feelings. They don't apologize because they don't see any reason to.

CHEAT CODES:

You could try going to the HR department, but there is a low chance you'll get any resolution. It would help if you have e-mails documenting your boss' bullying tactics, but this is hard because most bullying behavior happens face-to-face. Maybe HR will sit down with him and suggest he use an outside coach to work on his behavior. Unfortunately, unless the bully boss wants to change his behavior, this won't work. In fact, you may risk him taking it out on you even more.

Another approach, also risky, is to go to your boss' boss. If you have enough cred with him, he might listen to you and want to help you out. But you then have to live with your boss' reaction to you going over his head.

If your boss is bullying everyone on your team, maybe you can all go at him together in a show of solidarity. I've had no experience with this approach so I don't know what the chances are of success. At least this way, you won't be confronting the M.F. alone. Good luck with that.

Best approach is to stand up to this dictator. Assert yourself; let the bully boss know that he needs to find a better way to talk to you. You need to do this from the start—don't let him get in the habit of using you as a target, a doormat. Giving the bully awareness of his behavior is not enough—you need to help him by telling him how you want him to change. (See more in the section on Giving Feedback.)

COWARDLY LEADERS

Like the Cowardly Lion in the Wizard of Oz, some leaders are afraid to step up when they see something wrong, because they want to be liked. The cowardly leader will overlook it or ignore it because he doesn't have the balls to call a spade a spade. This is particularly bad when there's a problem with a staff member and the leader doesn't handle it. What happens is all the followers lose respect for the leader and everyone feels the impact of his inaction. A leader needs to take care of business right away. If he lets things fester and doesn't give immediate feedback, the consequences are huge for the entire team, maybe even the entire company. Some leaders are conflict-averse—they don't want to confront people with unpleasant conversations.

The cowardly boss wants everyone to like him. He is a people pleaser, so he avoids any and all confrontations. (See more in the section on Game Codes.) His personal motto is, "Why can't we all just get along." It's more comfortable for him to think, "It will blow over, and it will get better by itself." Every minute this leader doesn't take action is a minute of reputation destroyed. If an employee of a cowardly leader does something really bad—steals, lies or screws up a project badly—he will just sweep the incident under the rug. He can't even spell the word discipline.

You would think that a manager holds a leadership position, and therefore should help resolve conflict in the workplace. Woe unto you if you work under a coward. He will run away from conflict or escalate the conflict, making it difficult to work effectively. A cowardly manager cannot set or enforce rules of engagement in the workplace, making conflict resolution difficult.

As an employee of a cowardly leader, you won't get the support you need to deal with other departments. Your little coward leader won't be assertive with his peers or with upper management. He will back down from a challenge, wimp out, run scared, and hide. He will make a decision in private, then fail to stand by it in public if his plan goes sour. He will not take responsibility for his actions and instead will resort to the blame game. He will leave you alone in front of the firing line. He will not have your back. Even worse, he won't be the champion you need to get promoted.

I've coached quite a few weak leaders—cowards who are afraid to take a firm stand with their direct reports. Usually, the cowardly leader needs some tools and role modeling. He either hasn't ever seen what a good leader does—how he gives feedback, makes decisions, takes charge. Often a young person is given responsibility to lead and manage with zero training, zero support. I know that some cowardly leaders can be rehabilitated.

There is a space to be a good leader without being a tyrant. A courageous leader can be kind and be assertive, set boundaries and is seen as a force to be reckoned with. This is healthier than just being nice so people will like you, so you don't offend anyone. If a leader is too nice, he may be seen as desperate for approval, which will in turn cause people to take advantage of him. Some people are not born to be leaders, just like some people are not born to be parents. Fortunately, in the Wizard of Oz, the Cowardly Lion learned that he had courage inside him all along.

CHEAT CODES:

Keep your expectations low; the cowardly leader will not suddenly grow gonads and change into a strong leader.

You need to become self-reliant—you need to become the parent.

You'll have to take full responsibility for your own success. Don't wait around for a cowardly boss to help you.

Build your own reputation in the organization. This may mean going around him, but do what you've got to do to blow your own horn. I'm sure the coward isn't bragging about your good work to the powers that be. Just be careful that you don't cause your boss to be threatened in the process. It's a risky move.

Learn from the sad sack of a boss what not to do when you become a leader. The upside is you'll be wiser and stronger and a better role model when you become a leader someday.

If you and your teammates have a strong relationship, you can bond together and cover each other to avoid situations where your manager can point fingers, at least inside the department.

You could choose to stay close to the cowardly boss and help him succeed.

Show him your courage and let him rely on you to take on the tough battles.

Find ways to make him feel in control. When you have success, make him a part of it.

Make yourself indispensable to your department and to the organization. Maybe the cowardly boss will know he's safer with you than without you. You have to be willing to share the spotlight. If you're a confident, secure person, you can pull this off.

BOSS CHILD

Some bosses are like toddlers with power. They probably got promoted based on their technical knowledge or business expertise, but who have little to no emotional intelligence (IQ). These types of managers share traits with toddlers. They are stubborn, self-centered, pout, throw tantrums, demand what they want, and have short attention spans. They are emotionally immature—they can't control their feelings appropriately. Now we expect a two-year-old to be emotionally immature, but not the boss, who is supposedly a grown-up. For the boss child, the knowledge-to-emotional-intelligence equation is out of whack. I've made up these equations, just to make my point.

Just because a person has job knowledge doesn't mean he has the emotional intelligence to be leadership material:

My equation is: Knowledge IQ = 100 Emotional IQ = 25

Some people get promoted purely based on relationship with someone in power, even though they are lacking in both the job smarts and the maturity to lead others. Yikes! It gets exponentially worse. If you have to report to this childish loser, you are screwed. It happens. It's like giving a ten-year-old responsibility over the team. But this player is obviously highly skilled in playing the Ass Kissin' game to get ahead.

My equation is: Ass Kissin' = 300 Knowledge = 50 Emotional IQ = 12

I'm surprised at how many leaders lack emotional maturity. Don't be fooled by age or seniority or title—some people never grow up. Immature leaders come in all ages, so they can fool you with gray hair, but they are still children. They may wear suits or pearls but instead of silk underwear, they're wearing training pants. It's not enough to be a knowledge expert or a confident leader if you lack the emotional intelligence to understand yourself as well as others. Included in the category are the cowardly leaders, the tyrant leaders, and the bully leaders—all in some ways act like little kids. Leaders need to have empathy for others and be able to gain respect as well as technical or business expertise to get the work done.

Sometimes, an immature leader cares more about his personal gain than his employees—these leaders are narcissists. His beliefs, values and actions will eventually be a roadblock to success for himself and for his team.

Here are some attributes of immature leaders:

- They love to prove they're right.
- They throw tantrums when they don't get their way.
- They refuse to listen.
- They see their direct reports as a threat.
- They burn bridges.
- They are easily influenced by the wrong things or people.
- They will throw team members under the bus.
- They don't know how to build healthy relationships with their direct reports, peers, or senior leaders.
- They are inconsistent.
- They will micromanage.
- They crumble under pressure.
- They can't make the tough decision and show compassion at the same time.
- They don't care what people think.
- They have big mood swings.
- They are extremely territorial; they don't share well.

People bring all their psychological baggage to work with them—their childhood fears, their home life strife, and all sorts of things that don't serve them well in working interdependently. This is a huge problem when these weak people are promoted to lead others. Immature leaders are on a constant hunt to prove they are worthy. They love the spotlight and rarely share it with others. Immature leaders assume someone with an idea is jockeying for power or wanting their job. They assume every push back, suggestion or request is dissin' of authority. This causes them to label their followers by saying, "They just don't want to follow" or "Their heart is in the wrong place."

Sometimes, an immature leader won't delegate well because he thinks he has to do everything to prove himself. Of course, he believes he is better at everything than anyone on the planet, let alone anyone on his team. The immature leader will blame their actions on not having people who meet his expectations. Really? Well, I wonder whose fault is it that the team members aren't good enough. Or maybe, just maybe, there is a follower who is capable, but then, that would threaten the immature leader. He can't have good people around him who may show him up. You are bound to deal with an immature leader at some point, there's no escaping them.

CHEAT CODES:

Don't tell him he's acting like a baby. Remember he's a baby with the power to fire you.

Don't just endure his immature tantrums and behavior. If you do, you are part of the problem—an enabler. If your boss throws a fit, try distracting him or excusing yourself from the situation for a few minutes.

Stay in your neutral grown up place in your own head. You have to become the parent. Just quietly watch him act a fool and then strategize about how you're going to stay positive and find higher ground.

Use child psychology—set limits and give him kudos (or snacks) for good behavior. Don't let his bratty behavior get to you. When he's acting like he's in his terrible twos, you have to stay calm and let him vent.

Stay calm. Definitely don't try to be too rational or objective—that will really piss him off. Just be diplomatic.

Be a role model. Be calm. Be objective in the face of juvenile behavior by your boss.

Be proactive to try to head off any upsets. Learn what triggers him, anticipate, and act accordingly.

Try to stay positive, distract him (with candy? ice cream?) If you can.

Adjust to an unemotional stance—if you allow yourself to take it personally you will play right into his hands.

If you see a blow up coming, avoid him. Hide. Go outside. Give yourself a timeout since you can't give him one.

Reach into your manage up toolbox and take control as much as you can by being proactive. (See more in the section on Managing Up.)

Study his mood swings and choose your timing in communicating with the childish boss.

Don't take it personally when their mood swings. Remember, it's not about you. Kids get squirmy. Don't internalize it.

Once again, I see working with these folks as an opportunity for you to learn how not to be. Watch. Learn. Be better.

Questions to Consider:
- What other immature behaviors have you seen from managers?
- What other ways can you think of to deal with a childish leader?

MANAGEMENT VS. LEADERSHIP

There is a big difference. You manage things; you lead people. People follow leaders; they do what managers tell them to do.

Management things include planning, controlling, budgeting, forecasting, evaluating, and assigning the work. These things are task-based; they keep the machine moving at optimum efficiency. The problem in this thinking is that people are not machines. People need more than assigned tasks; they need purpose.

Leadership is about energizing people to accomplish a mission. Unlike a pure manager, a leader is not working just to keep a well-oiled machine in repetitive motion. True leadership inspires passion, purpose, and results.

The two go hand-in-hand: management and leadership. You need both skills to succeed.

MANAGEMENT	LEADERSHIP
Does things right	Does the right things
Has his eye on the bottom line at all times	Has his eye on the horizon
Plans detail	Sets direction
Focuses on systems	Focuses on people
Relies on control	Relies on personal power and trust
Has a short-range view	Has a long-range vision
Asks how and when	Asks what and why
Imitates	Originates
Accepts the status quo	Challenges the status quo
Organizes the workers	Nurtures workers' skills and talents
Has direct reports/subordinates	Has followers

Transactional style	Charismatic, transformational style
Seeks comfort	Seeks risk
Counts value	Creates value

People sometimes use the terms management and leadership interchangeably, without paying attention to the important differences between them. While managers are often in a leadership role, they may not necessarily go about their jobs as leaders—even if it would be better if they did. I believe that if you have people reporting to you, you need to be both—a manager and a leader. You have to get the work done through people and with a shared vision and motivation with your team.

Questions to Consider:

- Do you know a manager who is also a good leader?
- What have you seen that's different about a person who has both skill sets?

Co-Workers

BAD PLAYERS/SAD PLAYERS

Players are not just on sports teams. People at work are players, too. The good players make it a joy to be with them every day. They bring good energy and pump up those around them. Unfortunately, there are some bad players in the game, playing some wicked roles that you need to be aware of and have a strategy for how to deal with them. Wouldn't it be great if you could get a scouting report about these bad players in advance? "Today there will be two backstabbers, one ass-kisser, a blamer, and a narcissist at the meeting." Then you could prepare your strategy for dealing with these folks and not get blindsided by their antics. When you walk around assuming that everyone is a good person and in reality you're dealing with a bad player, that's when you get yourself in trouble at work.

Here are some examples of what emotionally immature players look like at work:

- They have no boundaries, filters, or common sense judgment.
- They whine or pout when things don't go their way.
- They blame others.
- They refuse to share resources.
- They storm out of the room, pouting and pissed off.
- They use a hammer to solve every problem; people are their nails.
- They're always negative.
- They set people up to fail.
- They are very dependent and needy.

You are going to run into these bad players at some point. Watch out and be prepared to deal with them. Bad players can be male or female and come in every shape, color, age and size. They can be at any level in the organization. You need to prepare and rehearse for that moment when you run into one of these knuckleheads. The alphabetical list:

Ass Kisser: This can be a male or female who sucks up to people, usually the boss, to get their way, to look good, and to make others look bad. This player can be very successful in certain situations.

Backstabber: He says one thing to someone's face and then says something entirely different behind his back. He smiles in your face but all the time he wants to take your place.

Ball Hog: He's that player on the basketball team who just dribbles and shoots and rarely passes the ball. He doesn't look around to see if someone else has a better shot. At work, he grabs up all of the shared administrative assistant's time or takes too much time talking in a meeting or holds onto information he should be sharing. He's way too selfish to share the spotlight. His motto is: "I got this; I don't need anybody else."

Blamer: He refuses to takes responsibility for his actions. He automatically assumes the fault is someone else's—it could never be his. His only concern is fingering someone and convicting him or her of his crime. Over time, no one trusts this guy anymore and he wonders why. Get a dictionary and look up the word accountability. The blamer wears a T-shirt that says: "It's not my fault."

Blocker: This guy has been around the organization a long time. He views his role as maintaining the status quo. His motto is: "If it ain't broke, don't fix it." He tries to keep new ideas suppressed because if the idea sees the light of day, he just knows it won't work. He actually believes he is doing the company a service, protecting it from the wasting time and money with those creative crazies who are trying to stir things up with their damn innovations.

Bull Shitter: He's not quite a liar, but he might as well be. He talks a lot of smack. No one is sure when he is telling the truth, exaggerating or just plain lying. He's good at setting people up who aren't wise to his game.

Buzz Killer: This guy takes all the fun out of work, quotes "the rules," threatens to tell the boss when he sees someone doing something wrong. His very presence drains the life out of the workplace.

Dirty Mouth: Every other word out of this guy's mouth is foul in the extreme. While our language has definitely gotten less formal over the years, at work some people just don't know where to draw the line. A woman with dirty mouth especially can get labeled and lose reputation points.

Dr. Jekyll & Mr. Hyde: He can be kind and encouraging one minute and vicious the next. Others are confused if they've only seen his kind side and will wonder who he is when he turns into his inner evil twin. This is a scary dude.

Gossiper: He loves to talk behind other people's backs. He spends way more time looking for ammunition on other people than doing his damn job. He is fundamentally so insecure that the only way he feels good is to make someone else look bad. And he has the nerve to pretend to be friends with his victims.

Hater: He walks around criticizing everything at work—products, programs, policies, people, and the work environment. He has an intense dislike for just about everything and everyone and he makes sure to share his negativity. He poisons the culture.

Hypercritic: If this guy ever smiles at something good that you've done, you're lucky. He reserves praise for absolute perfection. People around him learn not to hold their breath for praise. He hoards praise like gemstones because he needs to be the smartest guy in the room. He can't possibly compliment anyone else.

Imposter: He really doesn't even know what he's doing at work, but he's damn good at pretending to be competent. He cleverly gets people to do his work, hijacks other people's work, steals ideas, plagiarizes, and takes credit he doesn't deserve. Resume fraud perhaps?

Late Dog: He's constantly late for work or meetings, misses deadlines, or takes forever to return phone calls or e-mails. His thinking is, "I can be late, but you can't because you aren't as important as I am." This is a game of control. Being late is a way of messing with everyone else and feeling superior. But of course, he expects you to be on time and to respond right away to his e-mails and texts.

Liar: He manipulates the truth and uses alternative facts to protect himself, blame others, look good, and get his way at work.

Madman/Madwoman: Also known as crazy, lunatic, or maniac. He's all over the place. He likes to turn everything at work into a crisis. He may yell and scream and act up and throw things. He definitely says some crazy mean things to people. He seriously needs to chill. He drives everyone crazy.

Manipulator: He is a clever person who tricks people into doing things. He is the master of control, the puppeteer, and the con artist. Deception is his favorite strategy. He totally lacks the empathy gene. When he pats you on the back, you had better beware of what's coming next.

Motor Mouth: He just doesn't know when to shut up. He dominates meeting time; he slurps up all the air in the room. He rarely listens because he loves the sound of his own voice.

Narcissist: He is a self-important bastard (or bitch) who has an excessive need to be the center of attention. His motto is: "It's all about me. Always has been, always will be." He can be arrogant; he focuses primarily on his own needs. He can't spell the words empathy or sympathy.

Predator: He's looking for other people in order to use, control, or harm them in some way at work. He likes to make the kill and eat his prey. The Predator doesn't have to kill and eat you, though: he can just take you down with a smile. This person is the meanest of the mean at work.

Snake: He pretends to be nice but he's actually working against his coworkers. He's selfish and uses friendliness to mask his attempts to gain control. He steals ideas and takes credit for stuff that he didn't do. Beware of this guy: he's a snake in business casual clothing.

Superstar: He got this title from the higher ups—at least from his boss. He gets the limelight, the promotion, and the money and hey, probably even the girls (or guys) after work. Because he's getting all the shine, and he's likely arrogant as well, people don't like him except maybe the Ass Kissers. If he really has the goods, he may be able to wear this crown without backlash.

Questions to Consider:
- Do you see yourself here? Be honest.
- How would you handle one of these bad players if you knew in advance what their game was?

Sad Players—These folks deserve a shout out. They need to get it together or risk becoming one of the bad players when they get sick of being a sad player.

Invisible Work Horse: He is that hard-working person who gets no press and is therefore, taken for granted. He's actually invisible but he doesn't even know it. He thinks he's being a team player, but others see him as a submissive people-pleaser. Everyone assumes he doesn't need any acknowledgement. This guy needs to wake up and play the game.

Loser: He is that dumb person who just can't get anything right at work. He says the wrong things. He's a screw-up at work. He's pitiful and worthless, dragging everyone down. Everyone is wondering why he's even there.

Wimp: He walks around looking meek, mild, and afraid. He can't stand up to the boss or anyone else. And he's likely to become the poor innocent victim of pranks and blame at work. All of the Playground Bullies, Gossipers, Manipulators, Snakes, and Predators love to mess with him. He needs to man up and get some balls or he won't survive in the workplace.

Work Avoidance Technician: He hardly works at all but his lazy ass gets paid without breaking a sweat. He is the master of figuring out the minimum amount he can get away with. He creates a bad vibe for everyone else who is sweating it out. He might pretend to be a team player, but the truth is he's not really committed. He just needs to keep his paycheck. He's an Imposter posing as a team player. Maybe he feels he is more important than the team. The game is easy to spot. The slacker puts off unpleasant or difficult tasks until forced to confront them. Various excuses are used as delaying tactics. If your work depends on a chronic slacker, you are doomed to frustration.

GOOD PLAYERS—WHO DO YOU TRUST?

Ok, so you need to trust somebody at work. First and foremost, trust the people at work whose values align with yours. These are the kinds of things to look for in a co-worker, boss or cross functional team member—a good, trustworthy player.

- People who really listen to what you have to say—I mean sincerely listen. How do you know that someone is really listening? They ask you clarifying questions and show interest, even if they don't necessarily agree.
- People who do what they say they are going to do—who keep their commitments.
- People who encourage you and build on your ideas: "Hey, that's a really interesting way to think about that. And I bet we can add some other features."
- People who are direct, even if what they say doesn't feel good, at least you know where they are coming from.
- People who play well with others—who have mastered interdependency.
- People who admit their mistakes and accept responsibility—trust them.
- People who see you struggling to learn a new task or solve a problem at work and offer to help without you asking—trust them.

Receptionists, admins, tech support, and janitors are the true power in office buildings. Make friends with them and you can get anything you need or go anywhere you need. They really run the place. This is not brown-nosing; this is smart relationship management and networking. Don't be a snob—one of these folks could be just the mentor/guide that you need to give you the truth about the culture and office games, and help you to navigate the toxic waste puddles.

PLAYGROUND BULLIES AT WORK

This is that mean person at work who just messes with other people. As a child, he was that a young hoodlum who got off making the other kids miserable. On the playground, he used to take the ball away or trip the other kids. Now that he's supposedly grown up, he has a new playground, the workplace, and new targets—his workmates. At work he says mean things, sets people up, and generally intimidates and embarrasses others for sport. Some of the Bad Players are also bullies: Madman, Dr. Jekyll & Mr. Hyde, Backstabber, Snake, Predator, and Manipulator. Some bullies play the covert game—they are passive aggressive in their approach—so they don't look as overt as the other bullies (e.g. Manipulator, Backstabber).

Every workplace has a bully, sometimes more than one. Sometimes they form a partnership, fraternity, or even a gang in the office—"Workplace Crips." In this new adult playground, the bully puts his needs above the work—it's a turn-on to control someone else and make them miserable at work. Bullies can be men or women. It seems that female bullies target women most often as their victims. Men are equal opportunity in choosing their targets—both men and women. Bullies create a toxic work environment for everyone, even the witnesses or innocent bystanders.

Bullies are liars and cowards. They possess more anger than acumen. They usually rely on verbal abuse at work versus physical abuse because there's no law against bullying; there are laws against physical abuse, sexual harassment or intentional discrimination at work. So, you can bully your co-workers without any consequences.

There are so many ways bullying shows up at work that you may not recognize it. And it's exponentially damaging when the bully is the boss. Here are some common bullying mind games:

- Criticizing, always finding fault
- Stealing credit
- Yelling, screaming, cursing
- Blaming, accusing
- Discounting or denying accomplishments
- Threatening (job loss)
- Insults, put-downs, belittling comments, name calling
- Glaring, eye-rolling and other negative body language
- Humiliating
- Backstabbing
- Lying (about the target)
- Icing out (excluding)
- Constantly interrupting, especially in meetings
- Crowding personal space
- Intimidating gestures (giving the finger, slamming or throwing things)
- Complaining to the boss inappropriately
- Withholding resources
- Deliberately cutting out the communication loop (not sharing important information, not returning calls or e-mails)
- Discriminating
- Assigning meaningless duties as punishment
- Giving the silent treatment, ignoring
- Changing the rules, just for the target and denying privileges

All of these approaches are done in the name of control. The only way bullies know how to survive at work is to take someone else down. Some bullies get a kick out of acting out on their targets in public; other bullies prefer to do their damage behind closed doors. The wimpy bullies will tell you one thing to your face and then say something entirely different behind your back. Either way, these are sick games played.

Most bullies at work are opportunistic politicians. They read the cues and look for opportunities to climb up the ladder—but the ladder rungs are people's backs and they have the bully's cleat marks to prove it. The savvy bully makes himself well connected—he knows whose ass to kiss at work, usually the boss or the owner or someone up the chain. Not only does he kiss ass up the ladder to get ahead, but he also needs higher ups as allies to have his back. So when a victim tries to tell the boss about the bully's bad behavior, the boss (his ally with the thoroughly kissed ass) won't believe the bully is in the wrong. Kissin' ass works to keep the bully from getting the punishment he deserves for his bad behavior.

The bully believes it's all part of the game—careers are built on gamesmanship. He says, "It's the American way to get ahead—doing whatever it takes to get ahead, to win the game, loser!"

CHEAT CODES:

Don't ever blame yourself for how badly the bully treats you.

Take a stand from the beginning. Set boundaries.

Don't take any crap from anybody. Being disrespected is a not ok.

Don't back down. Don't be a victim. You have to care about yourself.

Give firm feedback. Rehearse what you are going to say. (See section on Giving Feedback.)

Be assertive, don't hedge your words or you'll sound wimpy.

If you need help, get some people on your side.

Don't appease the bully.

Avoid contact if you can. Don't respond to his e-mails, texts or phone calls.

Let him know your personal boundaries. Draw a line in the sand and tell him not to step over it.

Don't let him see you get emotional—don't cry in front of the bully.

Your boss can be a support, if you're lucky.

Get help from a counselor.

Don't talk to HR unless it's a legal issue such as sexual harassment. Otherwise, it's too risky because HR doesn't always know how to deal with the bullying issues. It could just get worse.

Realize that you can't change the bully—he is who he is. Karma will take care of his ass at some point.

Move on if you have to. It's not worth working eight to ten hours a day with this jackass.

MICROAGGRESSIONS

This is an invisible morale-killer in the workplace. Microaggressions are the somewhat hidden everyday verbal and nonverbal insults aimed at people of color, women, lesbian/gay/bisexual/transgendered (LGBT) persons, people with disabilities, religious minorities and others. It could be as simple as using the term "gay" when describing a piece of art on the wall or making a joke about where a transgendered person goes to the bathroom. It's likely that most individuals who deliver these detrimental messages are not even aware that they have done anything wrong. Sometimes these little acts are intentional, sometimes unintentional. On the surface, the words seem harmless or trivial but not to the person who is offended.

Microaggressions are like passive aggressive bullying. Demeaning a person, even ever so slightly, is really not cool. At work, where the majority tends to be white and male, people need to be more aware of the manure that comes out of their mouths.

CHEAT CODES:

Stay calm, even though your default is to slap them in the face. Take a deep breath. Pause. Step away if you need to.

Maybe give the offender the benefit of the doubt—the first time.

Ignore them if you can.

Don't laugh. Don't smile.

Challenge the validity of the person's statement: "That's not my experience and I don't think anyone else around here feels that way."

Lead them to the edge of the cliff and let them fall in by asking clarifying questions like: "Why are you so surprised that I'm a good presenter?" Force them to see their own biases without calling them out.

Just simply say, "That's not right." Or "I'm not ok with what you just said."

Don't call them names, though many good ones may come to mind in the moment.

Change the conversation.

Talk to someone you trust about the situation, ideally one of your peeps.

If you have a witness to the stupid insult, ask them if you heard the other person correctly, in front of the person who made the comment.

If you're brave enough to deal with the flak, you can document the microaggression and file a formal complaint with HR. It is illegal to discriminate.

Go ahead and flip out if it's that bad. You don't owe the fool any courtesy if they dropped a big bomb on you.

Do nothing. Sometimes you just have to let the hurtful comment go.

WOMEN AT WORK

Let me start by saying I have been privileged to work with some amazing women—as my peers, as my bosses, as clients, as direct reports. I have been fortunate. I wish I could say that this experience is the norm in work life, but I've heard from many women that my positive experiences with women are not the norm. While both women and men are capable of bad behavior at work, for some reason, females create drama in the workplace more than males. I am generalizing here, so I may not be talking about you, my sisters. But there can be catty female behavior that's just insidious—constant comparisons, talking about how someone is dressed, gossip, accusations, and jealousy. I've seen sorority girl behavior and cliques in the workplace, just like in school. All this emotional activity can be overwhelming and it's definitely unproductive. I don't often see the same male-on-male emotional behavior that I see with women.

Some of the most difficult consulting situations I've been in involved female managers managing other females. Women employees tend to run to the female boss to complain more than men do. It's unfortunately common for a female leader to find she spends more time dealing with drama queens than she would like to. I had an interesting conversation with a very high-ranking female executive at a board retreat about this very topic. I asked her what her experience was as a leader and manager of female employees. She was of Vietnamese descent, which you will see is relevant to what she told me.

"So many young women approach me, just suddenly want to ask for advice, career advice or emotional advice, family, boyfriends and these types of things. I'm like, I don't want to set a precedent to be your counselor, your girlfriend, your best friend, your home girl, your mama, or anything like that. You know, I have one mama and she's enough. She's an immigrant mama. But there's a big struggle there, an unfair expectation on women, that I don't think men get."

Then she addressed a male board member present at this conversation. She said, "You don't have your direct reports, women or men, running to you saying things like, 'I've got some personal issues going on and I'm going to have trouble meeting that deadline.' Do you? No. That just won't happen to you."

While I think it's great for women to have someone they can talk to, another female who can perhaps relate better to their circumstances than a man, this relationship can be tricky. Some women managers try too hard to be both girlfriend and boss. This strategy rarely works because it is really important to manage emotional distance. Female managers need to set clear boundaries with men and women, but the relationships they have with their female employees require special handling. If a female manager is too cold and demanding, they can push female employees away. On the other hand, if the manager is too mothering, she may invite too much emotional stuff into the relationship with female employees. It's such a complex challenge as a female boss, staying close enough to your staff so they know that you care, but distant enough to lead them.

Women in leadership roles need to keep in mind that there can be discrepancies between the behaviors that a man can demonstrate without negative consequences and those seen as acceptable for women. If a woman is too outspoken, assertive, or even angry at work, she could be judged differently than if those same behaviors are coming from a man. A woman may be called a bitch for coming across as too strong. A man doesn't get called anything or may even get a compliment for saying the same words, in the same tone of voice. On the other hand, if a woman at work shows compassion, she's considered soft—and that's not a good thing either. So, you're damned if you do and damned if you don't play the testosterone game.

CHEAT CODES:

Do your job and do it well. It's hard enough being female in the male dominated work world so stay focused.

Avoid the drama queens, even if it means you have few friends. Sometimes it's better not to join the sorority. Stay out of the cliques.

Build your own support group with positive, like-minded women and men. Surround yourself with professionally accomplished, stylish women versus hating on them.

Play to your strengths.

Don't fight over handbags.

Don't cry in the building, not even in the bathroom.

Stop being bitchy. Yes, I'm talking to YOU.

Stay out of the competitive fashion game.

Don't whine. Women just can't complain as much as men can at work. It's just not a good look.

If you're the boss, don't tolerate the bitchy behavior. No catfights allowed.

Empower other women. Help women; help each other progress through the corporate games.

Become bilingual at work. Hold your own in "guy talk." But don't lose your female language. Make sure your voice is heard at the big table.

Pick your battles carefully—the fewer the better with both men and women.

Don't dress like a slut, don't act like a slut, don't be a slut.

Confront the female gossips, especially if they are talking behind your back. Let them know it is not cool with you.

Don't be a gossip yourself.

Stay engaged in every opportunity to network. Go to the company happy hours and events. Watch your intake. Don't try to match the fellas, shot for shot.

NOT ACCOUNTABLE—WHO ME? WHAT?

Some people have the maturity or the courage to be accountable. Unfortunately, I see so many examples of people being unaccountable that I'm shocked when I see someone who is actually stepping up, taking ownership for their actions and holding others accountable for their actions.

It's all about emotional maturity. For some people, I know it's so much easier to blame someone else when there's a problem, or just ignore incompetence when you see it. Overall, not holding yourself or other people accountable for their actions sets low standards for the group or team. Everyone has a responsibility here:

- You – You've got to be emotionally mature enough to say, "I did it. I made a mistake. I own it and I will make it right." Your personal power will grow exponentially when you do this.
- The Leader - When you're the leader, you have to be publicly self-accountable and you have to hold all of your followers to the same standard. You can't let people get away with poor performance or bad behavior. If you duck your responsibility, you will lose all respect from your team and others in the organization.
- Your Peers – This is really hard—telling one of your peers that they have let you down or the team down as a result of their actions. When you're afraid to call one of your peers on their counterproductive behavior or disappointments, you allow a lose/lose situation to prevail. And if you don't man up to your teammate at work, I guarantee he will repeat the behavior.

Without accountability, mediocrity rules. Not holding people accountable for underperforming does them no favors—it misleads them and gives them the impression they can get away with not meeting expectations. Sometimes it's not until their annual performance review when they get an unsatisfactory rating that they get the message and that surprises them. On the best teams, members hold themselves and each other accountable.

I was in a budget meeting with my executive team members. As Vice President of Marketing, I was responsible for the budget for both Sales and Marketing. The Sales team pulled money out of my budget for "trade promotions"—discounts on products offered to the retail customers as incentives to run special pricing, put up end-aisle displays, etc. At the meeting, the head of finance raised the point that my budget was considerably overspent on trade promotions. I said, "That's Sales' fault, not mine." Finance guy said to me, "Do your job!" He was right. I was accountable for keeping Sales on track with their spending. At the time, I was pissed that he called me out like that in the meeting. He was doing his job—holding me accountable.

Sometimes, lack of accountability happens because there is no clarity about roles and responsibilities. This leads to a situation where when something goes wrong, no one comes forward to accept responsibility. When we fail to hold others accountable, we reap the consequences—some obvious, some not so obvious. A lack of productivity is one of the more obvious negatives that come to mind. While everyone is busy pointing fingers at each other, deadlines don't get met, the work remains below standard, or customers continue to be dissatisfied. Worse yet, things won't get better until people stop trying to blame and start addressing the issue that caused the problem in the first place. This cycle will continue until people take accountability for their contribution to the problem and focus on seeking solutions.

CHEAT CODES:

Accountability starts with clear expectations. Make sure you understand what is expected of you—the end results, the timeline, the investment, and the use of other resources.

Have clear objectives that can be measured easily. That way, you'll know if you're hitting the targets.

Define what success looks like in advance. Otherwise, you're shooting for a vague target.

Take responsibility for your actions.

Take initiative. Be proactive. Don't just wait to be told what to do.

Do what you say you are going to do. Keep your commitments.

When you see others not being accountable, call them on it. Don't let your peers, teammates, or others get away with not keeping their promises.

Communications

CATCHING SIGNALS

In baseball, the catcher and pitcher can't talk to each other on every at bat, so they use hand signals. If the signal is given too quickly, the pitcher may get confused. If the catcher's legs where he flashes the signals are opened too wide, the coaches from the opposing team can see the signs and relay the pitch to the hitter. That's why the positioning of the hands and fingers are critical. Think about how that analogy carries over to the workplace. If you're on the receiving end of the signals (pitcher), you need to know what they mean and how to react. If you're the sender (catcher), you need to be extremely clear in how you give directions (signals). Both of you must be on the same page. Clear communication is vital in any relationship, especially at work. The most productive teams share the same playbook. They clearly know what winning means and they have clear tactics on how to win, together.

Sometimes at work, people are not on the same page. One department may have its own agenda, regardless of the strategy of the team as a whole. Another department may be sending clear directions but the receivers aren't speaking the same language. Marketing speaks one language. Sales speaks another language. Distribution doesn't speak either language. Somehow, all these disparate functions need to come together, agree on the game plan, and use the same hand signals. If Product Development calls for product change and Manufacturing doesn't understand the adjustment, the product will turn out wrong. We have to be able to pick up each other's signals and use the same playbook.

Other signals that need to be understood at work are more subtle—how to dress, how to talk, what's funny, what's offensive, what behavior is tolerated. Some people just aren't that quick on the uptake—they either don't see/hear the signals or don't interpret the signals correctly. If you're lucky, you'll gain this sixth sense over time or you'll get a mentor who can teach you how to catch the signals.

CHEAT CODES:

Don't assume you know the internal signals in the workplace culture. The signals change with management changes and within and between departments.

Learn the signals in your workplace. When you change jobs, even in the same company, you need to learn the signals of the new subculture.

Talk to the folks who've been around a while. They can help you translate the subtle signals.

If you have the cred, call bullshit when you see it. Keep it real.

Help ensure that everyone is on the same page. Have people repeat what they've heard or demonstrate they understand in some way.

Try to be aware of the message you are sending in all situations.

Make sure what you say and how you say it match up.

Put your cell phone away. Close your laptop.

Dress the part. Make sure that "business casual" isn't "business careless." The old saying applies here: "Dress for the job you want, not the job you have."

This is old school, but a firm, confident handshake sends a strong positive message.

For women in particular, put your hand out there first to shake hands and shake it like you really mean business. I hate a wimpy handshake—from a man or a woman.

Look a person in the eye when you're in conversation. This is your best tool for communicating effectively.

When you're in a meeting, engage with everyone in the room.

Don't slump around like you're tired and old, even if you are. Stand up straight and walk with confidence.

Don't roll your eyes, give the finger, or fold your arms across your chest for long periods of time. It's not a good look.

Watch others for their nonverbal cues and adjust. People's body language and tone give you important information on how you need to adjust.

Learn the language of the other functions/departments you work with. Adapt to their special dialect.

Notice if someone is bored. Change it up.

If you work with people from other countries, do your homework. Every culture has different signals. You don't want to insult someone from Japan, for instance, by handing your business card face up.

92 COMMUNICATIONS: CATCHING SIGNALS

I didn't plan to have to this very basic level of advice giving until I read all ninety-five of the stories submitted to me for this book. Now for those of you who are true grown folks, you can skip this section. But for those of you who don't catch signals real well, or just want to see what's happening, here are some things you should never do at work. Any workplace. Anywhere.

Don't do these things at work:

- Women: don't bend over while wearing very short skirts with a thong or nothing. Maybe full-on underwear would work? Still no, on the bending.
- Don't have sex in the "quiet room"—designated for lactating mothers or people who are ill and need to lie down. And don't leave your condom wrapper as evidence. Just don't and don't.
- Don't watch porn in your cubicle on your break. Or at least turn mute on. No. Some companies monitor Internet behavior while on the job.
- Don't come to work drunk or high. Or smelling like you drank alcohol and/or smoked weed. Oh, and it's not ok to do either of these things before an interview. Word to the wise.
- Don't take a fifteen-minute smoking break every hour. Even with an e-cigarette. Even a vape pen. You may think you're slick but…. I don't care how high functioning you think you are, just leave the drugs and alcohol for off hours. And how are you going to explain your extreme case of the munchies during the workday?
- Don't talk about your sex life openly—waiting for a meeting to start, in the hallway, in the lunchroom, or loudly from your cubicle.
- Even though you are homeless, it is not ok to make a blanket bed and sleep on the mezzanine every night. Or take a shower in the company gym. Or keep all of your food in the lunchroom refrigerator.
- Don't hit on the women (or men) who work right next to you, especially not on your first day…or week or month… or ever.
- If you and your "boo" are having relationship issues, don't spend your time at work texting back and forth all day.

Everyone does appreciate that at least you're not talking on the phone where everyone could hear it. But still. Over-sharing. TMI – Too Much Information.

GAME CODES

With people, just like in video gaming, there are codes and equations. Learn these codes for handling conflict situations and to pick your battles carefully. Each number stands for an individual.

0 + 0 = 0

In this equation, we both avoid each other so there is no interaction. Some people are just uncomfortable with conflict, so they avoid dealing with any situation that involves disagreement or debate. What happens at work is that people avoid talking to each other at all on an issue because they both may be unsure of how to handle the conversation, be insecure, non-competitive or just plain shy. Conflict avoidance can be a good survival technique at work when the battle isn't worth it or you feel ill equipped with the tools to go into the battle. Avoiding conflict can be a lose/lose proposition. I lose because I didn't stand up for myself; you lose because you didn't stand up for yourself. And we both resent each other for whatever the conflict is that remains unresolved. In any event, you and I don't talk so there's no end result. Nobody came to play.

Score: Me = 0. You = 0. Total = 0.

0 + 1 = 0

This is another avoidance equation. In this situation, one of is willing to deal with the issue; one of us isn't willing or able to deal with it. Maybe we just put it off until one or both of us is ready to deal with it; that time could be never. If one of us feels it's too risky, that person will continue to avoid the situation, likely venting about it to others but refusing to deal directly—passive aggressive behavior. I came to play, but you didn't show up. Again, there's no end result. Score: You = 0. Me = 1. Total = 0.

0 + 1 = 1

This is like a gimme putt in golf—I let you have the win because the ball is close enough to the hole. At work, I let you win because: a) the issue is clearly going to end up in your favor, b) the issue isn't as big a deal to me as it is to you, or c) I owe you a win. Instead of competing for the win, you just let the other person do it their way—you accommodate them. Sometimes, it's best to give someone the win. If this is not the hill you want to die on, let your co-worker have the win.

Be careful. If you do this too often at work, you will get run over and you get a reputation as a wimp. Your credibility and influence will get lost if you keep playing this game. While you may believe in keeping harmony and peace, it's just not the way to go every time there's conflict at work. Accommodating can be like a Lose/Win situation where you act like a doormat and let the other person have his way with you. If you're being Mr. Nice Guy thinking it will get you points, that's probably not going to happen in a situation where everyone else is playing to win. A manager who is too accommodating will definitely lose the respect of his staff.

Score: Me = 0. You = 1. You win. Total = 1

1 + 1 = 0

There are several versions of this game.

Game 1: We both lose.

We're both all in, we compete for the win, but we both lose. In the workplace, this can mean that the wrong decision gets made, just because of bullying or one-upmanship. The person with the biggest bark gets their way and that way could be totally the wrong way. This equation is bad competition. When two people get together and they both leave with nothing—no shared agreements, no value added—that's a lose/lose situation. All the two of them have are hurt feelings and frustration.

Game 2: No-win
In game theory, a no-win situation is one where no player benefits because while two people have choices to make, none of the choices are favorable for anyone. No-Win is the same as being between a rock and a hard place.

Game 3: I want you to lose with me.
The attitude of lose/lose is: "If I'm going down, I'm taking you with me." Both parties lose, both parties fail.
Score: Me = 1. You = 1. Total = 0.

1 + 1 = 1
We both came to play, but only one of us wins in the end. Some people are highly competitive—they only play to win. That means someone else is always going to lose. The problem is, in the workplace, we need to be clear about what winning means. If two peers are competing against each other and their game is all about their egos versus getting the work done, then it's a bad competition. Unfortunately, this is a game that we're all taught as children. The problem is so-called grown ups have not stopped playing it because it's the only game they know. Now being competitive can be good as long as we are united in understanding the real loser is the outside—our company's competitors, not one another. Supposedly in the

workplace, we're all on the same side, working for the good of the whole organization. In reality, it often doesn't work out that way.

Score: Me = 1. You = 0. So 1 + 1 = 1

.5 + .5 = 1

We both come to play and end up negotiating on a compromise—each of us gives up something and we meet somewhere in the middle. Most people think that compromising is a good thing. Well sometimes it is and sometimes it's absolutely the wrong way to go. In a negotiation, compromise can be the best solution. If we're working on a project together, the compromise might dilute the end result.

When we meet in the middle, you got some of what you wanted, I got some of what I wanted, and it all works out for the best. The equation may not be 50/50 (e.g. 60/40, 45/55) but it adds up to 1, and that's better than 0.

Score: Me = 1/2. You = 1/2. Total = 100%

1 + 1 = .5 or .25 + .25 = .5

We're debating an issue and end up with a solution that is only a small portion of what we both came in with. It's a sadder compromise equation.

Score: Me = .25 You = .25. Total = .5

1 + 1 = 2

This is a win/win—when two people get together and they both walk away with a win. A win/win can only happen when the people involved can see benefit in having it turn out that way. If anyone is in this game for himself, it won't work—that person will be looking to make somebody a loser. It's admirable to go for win/win, if you have the right parties involved and the time to work towards that end goal.

Score: Me = 1. You = 1. Total = 2

1 + 1 = 3

This is a rare situation—people who are about coming together and creating something new that neither one involved could have possibly come up with alone. It's taking Win/Win to the next level. This is collaboration—we come together to discuss a solution or create a new product or service and when we're done talking, the end result is better and more than either of us. Collaboration is not about winning or losing, it's about inventing and innovating. "Synergy" is the result of true collaboration.

But here's the thing—collaboration takes a lot of time and selflessness. It means there will be no competition, no winning or losing. When true collaboration happens, it takes very special people who are patient, smart, willing to share, and commit a lot of time to find the best answer or solution. It requires transparency—the lack of hidden agendas. Not many people are willing to be this exposed in a conversation with others—about their business, capabilities, strengths and weaknesses. Collaboration requires emotional maturity—the ability to leave your ego at the door. You all have to be willing to move off your positions completely to get to this equation.

Score: Me = 1. You = 1. Total = 3.

SQUAD GOALS

Hollywood loves the underdog story—the plot where the losers win against all the odds. In the movie Star Wars, the Rebel Alliance was at a big disadvantage versus the dark side of the Force. They had less firepower, but they had passion and teamwork. In the movie Remember the Titans, despite dealing with racism and losing their best player, the high school football team won the state championship. In the film Cool Runnings, the unlikely Jamaican bobsled team overcame obstacles to win the Winter Olympics. You get my drift.

A team filled with the best players who can't get on the same page will flounder in mediocrity, while a team filled with run-of-the-mill players who communicate effortlessly will be contenders every year. Just like in sports, work teams that let their egos go and form a strong bond will succeed—and have fun in the process. When everyone is on the same page—from the president, to the managers to the supervisors from the all the way down to the lowest level, great things happen.

The best teams that I've seen have members who keep an open mind, listen to one another well and understand clearly where they are all headed—to the goal line. It's true in sports; it's true in the office. These teams, even when there is tension, can effectively navigate to common ground. They know that conflict is healthy and they know how to handle it.

It is easy and tempting for team members to blame team dysfunction on leaders' failure to lead. Not so fast. Teams are a collection of people who can choose to work well together, or not. Each person contributes to the chemistry and function of the team, and everyone is responsible for their own contribution. In the same way, great teams elevate everyone's performance, while dysfunctional teams tend to degrade each individual's performance.

CHEAT CODES:

Get to know the people on your team—as much as folks are willing to share. The more you understand each other, the better you will get along.

Do things outside of work with your team. Hang out.

Have fun in your team meetings. Even when it's a tough conversation, find some humor.

Have a shared purpose, something you can all rally around and be passionate about.

Make sure every player on your squad knows his role. Think about a football team where the defensive lineman has a clearly distinct role from the safety or defensive back.

Have simple processes for getting things done within the team. Keep it informal.

If possible, your work team needs to sit together. Even if it's a temporary project team, there is great benefit in housing people together. You'll get more done, communication will be easier and you'll develop the camaraderie and passion that great teams enjoy.

Build and strengthen trust. Work on it all the time.

Encourage diverse thinking on your team. Avoid groupthink—where everyone is too vested in getting along and there's no healthy debate.

Be brutally honest with each other; don't play the passive aggressive game. Call team members out on when they are full of it. Keep it real.

CORPORATE SPEAK

You have to learn the lingo—the special collection of abbreviations, phrases and words that are unique in your workplace. It sounds like English, but it's not a language anyone else knows outside of the place where it's spoken. Every time you change jobs, you have to learn the definitions all over again. If you don't get bi-lingual really fast, you will be left in the dust. Every organization has its own alphabet soup: government agencies, academia, nonprofits, companies and other institutions. Sometimes, the jargon gets ridiculous. (I recommend a book on this topic in the Resources section at the end of this book.)

In my first corporate job in the 80's, the word "niggling" was used a lot to describe the critique of a document for content and typos. (I hated that word. Very politically incorrect to some of us.)

Here are some common corporate buzzwords:

Amped – Like having a hard-on; so excited about a project or idea

Backburner – Putting something away to deal with later; actually this idea will probably never see the light of day

C-Level – The leaders at the top whose titles all start with the letter "C"(CPO, CFO, COO). Could also include the Senior Vice Presidents, and Vice Presidents.

Sacred Cow – A product, process or service that can't be questioned, even though it doesn't make money and is no longer relevant. Don't you dare suggest changing it or eliminating it! (I'm sure the Hindus never meant for business people to disrespect their religious respect for cows.)

Talent – An HR upgrade on the word "employee"; often used with humor behind closed doors.

Wordsmith – To edit a document; the word that should have been used by my early employer instead of "niggling."

The challenge with these business buzzwords is that some of them come and go, like the slang names of illegal drugs—marijuana, Mary Jane, bud. Why? Because business book authors make up these phrases and companies are always seeking some new concept to be the best. So you get these terms like "best practices" or "ideation" or "game-changing" or "bleeding-edge." Some of these terms stick around, some are just fads that die out when the next big book tour hits the airways. It's hard to keep up. And every company picks its favorite so you've got to stay on your toes. One way to be on top of this game is to watch for the best-selling business books on the New York Times list and read them all, if you are so inclined.

At one company I worked for, one of the many new terms I had to learn was "BHAG"—Big Hairy Audacious Goal, pronounced Bee Hag." I had been in two major corporations prior to working there and I thought I knew all the business lingo. I was wrong. Our Big Hairy Audacious Goal was: "To build and open a new store every business day to achieve X number of stores by the year YYYY." Then to support the BHAG, we had these "base camps"—little goals that would get us to the mountaintop by the year YYYY. And then there were leaders in the company who were identified as "Sherpa guides"—the experienced corporate field commanders who would get us through the snow and blizzards of the mythical mountain. It was all very inspiring and colorful. Except when you were in a blizzard and there was no Sherpa guide to be found. Then you were on your own to get your part done. Well, that's the way I remember it anyway! Amazingly, we actually exceeded the goal and opened X number of stores before the goal date!

(Note: The term BHAG came from a business book that was published in 2004, Built to Last: Successful Habits of Visionary Companies, by James Collins and Jerry Porras. Weird thing is, I remember we used this term long before the book was ever published.)

Swearing at Work…Is It Ok?

Curse words have become part of the everyday language in life—in the media, in movies, on television and in literature. Politicians talk about whose ass to kick. Words that used to be inappropriate in public are now totally acceptable. So it's pretty common to hear the occasional f-bomb or other swear words at work.

Whether or not swear words are ok really depends on the culture of the organization. In some places, some four-letter words are just a part of the workplace vocabulary and it seems the more you curse, the cooler you are. Just be careful about cursing at work—it might damage your reputation if it's with the wrong people or taken the wrong way. If your boss curses, then you can assume it's ok with him; but don't assume it's ok with all the other managers and senior leaders. If I was just starting at a new company, I would hold off on the swear words until I observed how people talked. Bad language can be a turnoff or it may be celebrated in the workplace. You'll have to make that call. For those of you who may need some help, here are a few alternative ways to cuss nicely: fiddlesticks, frigging, shenanigans, witch, son of a gun, shucks, darn, crap and geez Louise.

When I was in the workplace, I really had to watch my mouth because, as you can tell, I am a big fan of swear words—they really help me make my points and convey a clear message. Where I grew up, it was part of survival, the rhythm of the 'hood. So I've learned to censor my language to be civil and respectable. In this regard, I consider myself bilingual.

CHEAT CODES:

You have to speak the language in your workplace, just try not to overuse the jargon. It's annoying.

Be yourself. Don't sell your soul to the corporate language devil.

There are many ways to impress people at work without speaking totally in corporate language.

Sometimes at work, the only f-words you should use are finance, forecast, fiscal (year) and five o'clock.

Ask for feedback on how you're doing with the way you speak and write at work. Don't assume you've got it all down perfectly.

Use stories; they're better than jargon at getting the point across.

All facts are boring. Lighten up with some humanity.

Be funny. Be appropriate. Humor conquers all.

Swearing is ok in certain situations; just don't do it constantly.

Find interesting ways to get people's attention at work with your presentations. Be creative.

If you hear someone overusing the corporate lingo, call him on it. But only if you have a good relationship with that person.

Questions to Consider:
- Do you know all the special words and phrases at your workplace—those words that probably don't get used anywhere else in your life?
- Can you hold your own in a meeting with the senior leaders—speaking the corporate code words?
- Is it a problem to curse at work?
- Can you swear in front of anyone at work or just among your peers?

BUSTED MESSAGES

Conversations need to be a more important part of how we get things done at work. Even with e-mail, at some point, you need to have real conversation. The reality is that face-to-face conversations maximize messaging. You get the whole bundle, body language, eye contact, and a chance to respond in real time. I'm not a fan of long e-mail or text messages. I say, handle your business in person; you'll save everybody a lot of time (you, the writer and me, the reader). All communication options are not created equally and need to be judged depending on importance. Here is one view of the communication hierarchy:

1. Face to face
2. Telephone call
3. Personal Letter
4. E-mail
5. SMS, MMS
6. Social Media 'DM' direct message, e.g. Facebook, Twitter, Instagram, Wall postings, comments, "Like," "Poke"

While face-to-face and phone conversations are the higher levels of communication, there's still room for a breakdown because one of you is:

Constantly interrupting—not really listening because his brain is too busy forming opinions and jumping in, sometimes completing the other person's sentence for them. The other person shuts down.

Autobiographical—jumping on his own long-winded tale of the time he experienced the same thing you're trying to describe. The other person blocks out the blah, blah, blah.

Multitasking—talking while working on the computer versus giving the other person the attention they deserve. The other person senses this and gets pissed.

Rambling—just can't seem to get to the point or maybe you don't even have a point. The other person blocks out.

Defensive—so busy explaining his actions that you aren't really listening. The other person didn't really need to hear this.

CHEAT CODES:

Make more time for face-to-face contact.

Pick up the damn phone and talk to somebody. Enough with the texts and e-mails.

Pay attention to who you're talking to and adjust your style to him. The responsibility is on you.

Be a better listener. That means stop all the back conversations going on in your head and be fully present.

Ask lots of questions to show the listener you're interested and really paying attention.

Repeat what you hear just to make sure you've really understood.

Count to five before you respond, if you know you tend to draw quick conclusions.

Talk slowly, like President Obama did in his speeches.

Make eye contact and hold it. Stop looking at your damn cell phone.

Watch your body language. Things like crossing your arms send a negative message, even if your words are saying otherwise.

Be brief and specific—even when you're telling stories.

Make sure you're having a two-way, not a monologue. If you're dominating, it's not really a conversation. Stop and breathe.

Questions to Consider:

- When have you experienced a communication breakdown?
- Can you analyze why it happened?
- Who do you know that is really pleasant to have a conversation with at work? What makes that person good to talk with?

E-MAIL CAN BE EVIL

E-mail is a great invention! No more writing letters and "sending them snail mail." It's efficient, but often e-mail gets misinterpreted and misused. A lot. The problem with e-mail is that you don't get the whole package. You can't hear the tone of voice that the writer is using, so you're left to assume tone. That can be a problem if you assume some emotional undertone. Sometimes it's the writer's fault; sometimes it's the reader's fault. (You know what they say about the word "assume:" it makes an "ASS" out of "U" and an ass out of "ME.") The writer can cause an emotional response because he:

- Uses too many exclamation points (!!!) or ALL CAPS or bold
- Tries to be funny and the reader doesn't share his sense of humor
- Assumes the reader has all the same information he has
- Copies the reader's boss or someone equally inappropriate
- Hits Reply All and copying too many people, probably the wrong people in the loop
- Says what he doesn't have the guts to say in person

CHEAT CODES:

Sometimes you just shouldn't say certain things in e-mail. Remember once it's sent, it's out there for life. Avoid these:

Personal emotions – "I'm mad at you," or "You pissed me off today."

HR actions: "You've been fired/demoted."

Vulgarities – "Wow, you really fucked up today."

Incriminating comments/gossip—"Did you hear that Jonathan might get fired for sexual harassment?"

Confidential or financial information—"Our department doubled sales last month but the company still didn't meet the market forecast."

Your salary benefits—"Dude I just got a $15K raise and I'm eligible for the twenty percent bonus pool now."

Spiritual or religious comments that are negative—"Did you see that dude Jake wearing his yarmulke to work?"

Racist comments...even as a joke—"Did you see that new Asian chick, Trisha that started today? You know they're all really smart."

I'd like to say use common sense when writing e-mails but it's clear that some people don't know what that means or have a definition that is shady. Maybe it would help you to think of your grandmother or mother reading your work e-mails, or having your e-mail message blasted on social media.

CHEAT CODES:

Write e-mails in reverse.

First, write the body.

Second, write the subject to match what you've actually said in the body.

Third, add the recipients last so that you don't accidentally send it before it's done.

Feel free to use the DELETE key. Hold it down. Doesn't it feel good? Less is more.

Spellcheck is NOT your friend.

Read it again before you push Send.

Think about all the possible ways the reader might interpret your words.

WORK TEXTS

You're probably texting more than you actually talk. Texting has replaced phone conversations and even e-mail. Texting is legit, when both parties are cool with it, but it requires judgment and skill. You can at least ignore a late night e-mail, but a text is more in your face. A text grabs your attention in a way that's hard to deny. Question for you: Is it ok to have your boss text you about work on your personal phone? I guess it depends on the job and the boss. So it's a Saturday night, you're chillin' with friends and you get a text from your boss:

Boss: Hey u need to revise the sales pres with the new mkt data that came in yesterday
You: OK you need it Mon am?
Boss: No on Wed is fine

You think to yourself: "Did dude really need to hit me up on a Saturday night?" Ok, I get that the boss wants to save himself the trouble of jotting a note to himself and referring to it later. By sending you a text, he can check the issue off his mental list. But now he has cut into your personal time—big buzz kill. Now the ball is in your court to remember the issue and take care of it. It's still the weekend but now you're thinking about work already; your weekend time got cut short. Come on, if he doesn't need to see the analysis until Wednesday, couldn't he have asked for it on Monday morning in the office? Was it really that urgent? This is textual harassment!

If your boss is a control freak and uses texts as a tool, that's not ok. Then texting becomes a form of harassment, especially when your boss is impatient for your response and keeps sending multiple texts, getting increasing snarly about you not getting back to him right away. Some bosses feel the need to have you prove that you are all in—totally dedicated to the job. He or she will try to make you prove that you live and breathe the work 24/7.

CHEAT CODES:

You need to set some parameters, make some agreements about texting with your boss.

Maybe your whole team needs to get together and agree on texting etiquette—at work and outside of work.

Before you send a text to folks you work with, ask yourself, "Is it really important or urgent?" Be respectful of interrupting someone else's flow.

You also need to be careful about texting while you're at work.

Texting during a team meeting is really not a good look. It's particularly annoying when folks are expecting you to be engaged, but your head is down. Some of us think you are staring at your own crotch area—this goes for women and men. Head up, eyes up, pay attention.

If you spend more time on your personal device texting with family and friends instead of doing your work, you will not do well. Texting can be an addiction so if you can admit you have a problem, maybe you need to tell your close friends and family not to text you during work hours, unless it's really critical.

Questions to Consider:

- What's your opinion of work texting? When is it ok, when is it not ok?
- Have you experienced textual harassment?
- Is it ok to use emojis in a workplace text?

Organizational Maneuvers

MEETING AFFECTIVE DISORDER

When I was working, if I got an invite to a meeting with no agenda attached, I wouldn't go. I found most meetings were a waste of time even with an advanced agenda. Somebody would do all the talking and the rest of us would just sit there. Not much interaction. And I was especially irritated if it was stuff that could have been easily put into an e-mail.

Sometimes, there are very good reasons to call a meeting:
- To take advantage of multiple brain power to solve a problem, brainstorm new ideas or build a project plan
- To discuss a deal with a partner, customer, or client
- To convey very sensitive, confidential information that should not be in writing (no e-mail trail)
- To give feedback or discuss performance (this would just be two people)
- To celebrate success

I worked with a project manager, a snarly old guy, who taught me some of the best lessons I've learned about meetings. He would lock the door at the exact start time of the meeting and if you showed up late, you were out of luck. This applied to everyone, even me, and I was the co-meeting leader. If he felt like unlocking the door at some point, he would write the names of all the folks on a board called "Late Dogs." He ran a tight, productive meeting, always. And no one dared come unprepared—he would lay you out verbally in front of everyone. An extreme approach, but effective.

If you look around at the number of people sitting at the table during a meeting, estimate their hourly salaries and do the math, you'll find the cost in dollars is scary. (This was one of my favorite past-times when I was sitting in a boring meeting.) So if the meeting is boring and very few people are actually engaged, it's no wonder that you look around and see everyone checking e-mail or texts or doing something on their laptops. Just imagine how much real work is not getting done during that hour-long meeting. Now multiply this by eight hours for the dreaded "retreat"—an all day offsite meeting.

CHEAT CODES:

The point is to use everyone's time wisely.

Before you set up a meeting, ask yourself if it's really necessary. If the objective can be achieved through some other means of communication, don't have a meeting.

Be really clear about the expected outcome(s). The purpose of the meeting should be at the very top of the agenda.

- *Make a decision*
- *Brainstorm to generate ideas*
- *Solve a problem*
- *Create a project plan*
- *Get status reports (only if this results in discussion, otherwise I say do this via e-mail)*

Have a reasonable agenda, by that I mean, don't overcrowd it. Give enough time for each topic, allowing for discussion. List agenda items in priority order, in case you run out of time.

Send the agenda out well in advance and invite input from those who are attending. It's better to know that others have issues or agenda items in advance versus having the meeting get off track.

Make the expectations clear so people come prepared.

Make sure the right players are in the room—the people who can actually make contributions to the discussion.

If necessary, have a timekeeper—someone who is tough enough to tell people they need to shut up. Another idea is to use a sand timer to limit the motor mouths.

Do a quick summary at the end—key decisions made and next steps.

If it was a big meeting, debrief the meeting. Do a simple +'s/-'s chart—what went well with the meeting, what did not go well with the meeting. The reason for this is so future meetings will be better.

Questions to Consider:

- When you attend a meeting, are you clear about the desired outcome before you get there?
- Does the meeting get debriefed? (What went well, what could have gone better?)

- Is the agenda managed well? Is there someone who keeps the time on schedule?
- Does the meeting get sidelined, that is, going down a path that wasn't on the agenda?
- Are next steps clearly identified at the end? Is there follow up?

OFFSITE RETREATS

An offsite is like an away game in sports. Sometimes the coach only takes the top players, the traveling team, and leaves the freshmen or practice players at home. At work, the away game may include just the senior management team or some assortment of cross-functional players. Or it could be an intact functional team. Often the offsite is an eight- to ten-hour day or days of grueling minutia or boring report outs when it should be a chance to get really creative and visionary with the team.

These sessions go by the name of Leadership Summit, Executive Session, Annual Planning Meeting, Global Summit or something similar. Some organizations spend tons of money transporting people from all over the country or the world to meet for two to five days on end—and this is not counting the thousands of dollars in salaries sitting around the table. Rarely is there a genuine exchange of ideas, collaboration or innovation at the offsite retreat. This is the sad truth. If you're going to spend all the time and money, why not make it worthwhile for everyone and the organization? Don't do it just because it's always been done. Or at least, change it up.

I've facilitated numerous events where the management team or a functional department takes a group to a neutral location—A hotel conference room, a resort or some other venue—for the purpose of annual planning, strategizing and/or team building. I can say with pride that the events I facilitate are productive and fun. I wish I could say that about all such events, but I can't. This is my sweet spot as a consultant.

CHEAT CODES:

Participants should leave the meeting feeling re-energized, re-motivated, enthusiastic and stoked. Here are my thoughts on planning an offsite retreat that rocks.

Good Planning—Be really clear about why you are having an offsite meeting. I like to get input from all the participants before hand—topics for the agenda, activity suggestions, gripes about previous sessions, etc. Input from others helps to set a good agenda.

You won't be able to please everyone, but you'll know what's on their minds about the offsite.

Light Agenda—Keep it manageable. Choose just a few really important, provocative topics; don't cram in eight topics. Be generous with the time allowed for each subject. This is the hardest part when I'm working with a client. The desired agenda is always overcrowded and I have to prune it back—it's painful but necessary. Figure out what is absolutely critical to discuss.

Timing—Maximum eight-hour days, six-hour days are even better. People get tired and bored sitting in a room all day with each other.

Engagement—Have activities and exercises that force every single person to contribute. No slackers allowed.

Distractions—No cell phones or laptops allowed in the session. Warning: some people, the device addicts, will get the shakes. I often provide Legos and other toys on all the tables for this purpose. Plus some people learn and think best when they are using their hands. These people are called kinesthetic learners.

Breaks—Allow longer breaks, at least fifteen to twenty minutes so the addicts can get their fix of e-mails and texts.

Number—It's hard to have an effective session with a really large group of people. Draw the line at the critical few.

Expectations—Send out several e-mails before the event, clarifying the purpose and outcomes, any pre-work required, participation and logistical issues so folks come fully prepared.

Discussions—Include lots of opportunities for interaction, debating and arguing. That's what I like to see in an offsite retreat. If it's just a bunch of reporting out or listening, who cares?

Close with Gusto—Have definite next steps identified with responsibility and timing attached, even for the sideline topics that came up. Always, always debrief the session to learn what went well and what didn't—learning to absorb for future offsite meetings. Have some celebratory moment to acknowledge all you have accomplished!

Team building—Don't call it team building unless you're going to devote significant time to these kinds of activities. Squeezing in a game of volleyball isn't team building. Team building involves debriefing an activity to mine for learning. I believe you need at least half a day to really do proper team building.

Free Time—Golf, tennis, using the spa. Allow time for these fun activities but don't put it on the agenda or call it "teambuilding." It's good to allow downtime for folks to do whatever they want. Some people will just go back to their room and check e-mails or do work and that's their choice.

> Location—Of course this depends on your budget. Make sure it's easy and convenient for participants to get there. You don't need to take people to the most expensive hotel in town to make them feel special. And do consider the optics of where you hold the retreat. The rest of the organization will judge.

Post-Offsite

Now here's my biggest concern—what happens after the offsite? If the spirit and the end products of the event are not kept alive, then it was a total waste of time and money. I hate to see that. The leaders and all the "traveling team" need to keep the momentum going by: a) reporting back to the rest of the organization about the outcomes, b) ensuring that the next steps/action items are followed up on and completed, and c) keeping all promises made at the session. If these things don't happen, it's a big letdown to everyone—those who attended and those who didn't. As a consultant, I don't get to stick around to see this process, but I do check in periodically with the leader to ask how it's going. I hate to have my name associated with an event that was awesome and then fizzled after the fact because of poor follow-through.

One of my favorite uses of an offsite retreat comes from Phil Knight, in his book Shoe Dog. Back in the days when Nike was struggling, around 1976, Knight would hold a periodic retreat with his top team leaders called "the Buttface" to discuss major issues, solve problems, and make strategic decisions.

> *Buttface referred to both the retreat and the retreaters, and it not only captured the informal mood of those retreats, where no*

idea was too sacred to be mocked, and no person was too important to be ridiculed, it also summed up the company spirit, mission and ethos.

I particularly liked the fact that Knight could find humor in the midst of a very trying time for the company during these sessions.

I can see myself so clearly at the head of a conference table, shouting, being shouted at—laughing until my voice was gone. The problems confronting us were grave, complex, seemingly insurmountable...and yet we were always laughing.

I wish I could have been on his team and at a "Buttface" retreat. I love that there was essentially a free-for-all to openly discuss any topic and that no hierarchy existed. Most of all, they had fun and could totally be themselves. If all offsite retreats were like this, the world would be a better place.

Questions to Consider:

If you've ever attended an offsite retreat...
- Describe what went well, what you liked about it.
- Describe what you didn't like about it. How could it have been better?

THE REORG

Sometimes this event is also called downsizing or right-sizing. Beware the rumor or announcement of a planned reorg—it can be a shifty move by the powers that be. Management decides to rearrange the players on the chessboard, create new departments, change people's titles and reporting relationships. The reorg is supposedly an effort to improve the way things run, but often it's a just convenient way to get some people under the cloak of getting leaner and meaner. Sometimes the reorg is done to appease the shareholders, to show rejuvenation; sometimes it's done to keep the company from tanking. Most of the reorgs I've seen and heard about have been absolutely futile, some verging on out-and-out disaster. The worst case is when the CEO reorganizes multiple times during his tenure, causing undue pain when he is really the problem. Instead of true, meaningful change, the reorg usually results in upsetting the natural workflow, putting everyone on edge, and deflating morale.

Just when you were getting comfortable with the dysfunctional processes so that you could feel fairly confident in how to get things done, the management team takes the Legos apart, pours them on the table and rebuilds a new structure. Immediately after the reorg, no one knows how to navigate, how to get anything done, who makes decisions, or whether they should feel stable again, ever. If you're lucky, the coffee rooms will still be in the same place. Morale sinks, unless you got lucky and somehow got promoted in the shuffle. Ha! Don't get your hopes up. The thing is, even though you knew the place needed to change, you really knew how to navigate and deal with it just fine the way it was. It's like being married to a jerk who suddenly finds religion and changes his ways but you wish he had just stayed the jerk you knew. You could handle that fool, but not this new evangelist who sleeps in your house.

Basically, after the re-org settles in, if you're still employed there, you'll find that you're playing the same work games with new position titles but it's the same old games. See the section Duck & Cover under Bad Office Games. In this case, Duck & Cover is a good survival strategy to save your spirit from the organizational shell game. The term reorg conjures up fear for many, and fear of losing your job is the worst feeling of all.

A Good Reorg

Is there really such an event? Yes. Now to be fair, sometimes a reorg can turn out to improve operations such as centralizing functions from disparate departments into one department like finance. I've seen some successful reorgs where the end result is truly remarkable, but even these are not without some pain and tears. The leaders of the effort need to communicate much more often than they may think is natural. They need to tell employees what is happening, what they're considering and why and get employee feedback at some level. If communication isn't managed well, the result will be fear, dread, paranoia, and drops in productivity. The rumor mill alone will drive some people to flee for safety and leave the company—and these people could be the "keepers."

People need to know that they are valued, even those who may not make the cut. The leaders have to be very clear about what will change and what will not change. Hopefully, some things, the foundational things—the company's values, the focus on customer service, the way people are treated—will remain stable, so people have something familiar to hold onto. A successful reorg needs incredible communication and planning, and most of all, the people involved need to be fully engaged in the process. Somehow, leadership has to convey the change in a way that excites staff, especially all the managers and supervisors. After all, it's the employees who need to keep the machine running even while the machine is in the pit getting an oil change.

What I've seen happen is that while the reorg design team—which usually includes HR—is behind closed doors mapping out the plan, leaks occur. The word gets out, despite the "pinky swears" among the reorg team. And the word is not good to those outside the room. Then management has to go into spin control mode—it's ugly, messy, and sets the whole effort up for a bigger uphill battle. For this reason, I propose an initial message with a broader audience to at least acknowledge that change is being considered. I know this level of openness is risky and it won't work in every organization, but it's a better approach in the long run than keeping the whole reorg a secret and then issuing a proclamation with the new org chart and new work processes. This effort takes a lot of time and commitment from all the leaders—it needs to happen early in the reorg design.

Here are some ways to manage the reorg game well.

CHEAT CODES:

Get the right people involved early in the process.

Set up small focus groups with supervisors to understand what is working well and where they see opportunities for improvement.

Send out feedback surveys to capture what the lower level folks feel is really working well.

Be very sensitive to what staff is saying— upper management reads their input as, "Don't mess with this."

Seek full input from staff. Management that allows this process to happen may be pleasantly surprised.

Management may get some really good ideas and feedback

Include some important stakeholders outside the organization—top customers or vendors—who could contribute to a great outcome.

Create ambassadors of the reorg plan. The employees who get to participate in the process become the best ambassadors of the reorg plan.

It's often the first level supervisors who will have the most impact on how well or not well the reorg is received.

Identify who the other most influential people are downstream—the good players that everyone else respects and goes to—even if some of these folks are line workers.

The right messaging is critical; in fact, the communication plan may deserve some outside help.

Share the facts that are driving the reorg plan— marketplace changes, budget constraints, new technology—they can then open the discussion to a broader audience to generate suggestions.

Staff may be more likely to buy-in with some of management's thinking.

Change makes people uncomfortable. Period. It upsets your patterns and habits. But if you're going to stay employed, you need to adapt to the shift in organizational structure, the new boss, the new demands. Give the change time to settle in; a snap reaction isn't going to make the change easier for you. Be skeptical about organizational rumors—get the facts. Talk to your manager and others inside and outside your department to try to understand the new org as best you can. The more you understand, the more you may be willing to go with the flow of the new approach. Try to see the possibilities in the new situation. Realize that there's more than one way to get things done and the new reorg might just improve things. You can survive the reorg and any other changes that come your way. You really can. I've survived several reorgs—centralization, decentralization, different reporting relationships, and physical moves—and I'm here to tell you, it can be done. You can handle anything with the right mindset.

Questions to Consider:

- Once I get beyond the temporary pain of the reorg, will I still be proud to work at this company?
- Is my new role something I can be equally happy with?
- Can I see the light at the end of the tunnel?
- What are some new possibilities coming out of the reorg?

Super Powers:
The Biggest Cheat Codes You'll Need

PERSONAL POWER

When you're in charge of others officially, that is, they report to you and you can decide their fate, you have position power. You have power because of your title. You can direct others, impose penalties, threaten livelihood and reward performance. Most people aspire to have this kind of power, but it is not always the most effective power, especially if it is abused and causes fear. Parents, coaches, teachers, bosses, and superheroes have position power. Here are examples of what position power sounds like.

"Just do it, because I said so. No questions asked."

"If you don't do it my way, you can leave."

"I don't have to rationalize it. I'm in charge."

The tyrant leader would say all of these things with authority. He would not have to rely on personal power because he could use intimidation and position power. This is the dark side of the Force and not where most of you want to be. The best leaders I know get people to do things because of their personal power, not their position power. People respond better to personal power.

When you have no official power, but you need to influence others, you call on your personal power. This is the kind of power we all possess, regardless of our title, and it is the best kind. Whether you are a project manager or an administrative assistant, you have other people who you need to depend on and direct without being their boss. We all have personal power and access to the Force—to use for the good. Everyone has personal power, but some don't know how to build it or use it. When you tap into that power, people will want to be influenced by you. They will seek you out. People will follow you or do what you ask because they respect you and know that you appreciate their efforts.

You build your personal power by building credibility and trust.

CHEAT CODES

Here are some behaviors you need to build your personal power.

You do what you say you are going to do—keep your commitments/promises.

You listen fully to what other people are saying and you confirm or clarify to ensure that they feel correctly heard.

You have a can-do attitude.

You are honest and forthright with people.

You take responsibility for your own mistakes. You don't blame others.

You convey confidence.

You are considered a knowledge expert in your area and you objectively evaluate relevant facts and information.

You carry your share of the workload and more. You reach out to help others.

You can maintain a sense of humor, even when things are tough.

You remain calm under stress.

You are open to new and different ways of doing things.

You cannot abuse or overuse the words "please" and "thank you."

If you find yourself running late for work, pick up some donuts or muffins. Then you're not the person who's late, you're the person who brought breakfast!

To be successful in your career, you need to be able to influence other people. This involves developing personal power. You will want people to think positively about what you do, listen and accept your ideas, and also do things that you need them to do. Without the ability to influence others, you can't get much done at work. Your personal power is your superpower. I want you to have super personal powers that give you influence and respect in the organization—no matter what your position title.

Questions to Consider:

- Is there something about your swag that attracts people to you at work?
- Why do people do what you want them to do?
- When you are being successful, what is it that you do that gains cooperation from others?
- What connections do you have that people value?

THE GIFT OF FEEDBACK

Believe it or not, feedback is a gift. Now you may not like the gift, but you take it and you say thank you. Maybe you will realize later that it has value, but not in the moment you receive it. Without feedback, how do you know what you're doing well, what you should keep doing, what you're not doing well, or what you should stop doing? You need to know these things so you can understand how you're being perceived by the people you work with. Most of us are uncomfortable with getting feedback, especially if it's negative. Some people can't handle constructive feedback—they automatically default to it being negative. And a few people can't even handle positive feedback—they just can't take a compliment. Why is this? I don't know for a fact, but I believe we just don't learn how to give or receive feedback very well when we are young—from our families or from our teachers. I wish this topic was formally taught and practice was required.

Messed Up Feedback:
- Starting with "You"—this word signals a personal attack and invites immediate defensiveness. It sounds like an accusation. This is a bad beginning: "You are always late to staff meetings." This is better: "I feel annoyed when you are late for staff meetings."
- Don't use labels—"You're irresponsible and a slacker, dude." This is better: "I felt annoyed when you missed the deadline we had agreed to."
- Don't exaggerate—"You're always late for deadlines." The words "ALWAYS" and "NEVER" are guaranteed to kick start

an emotional backlash. You might as well have added, "idiot" at the end.
- Don't be judgmental—Avoid words like "good, better, should, bad." "You should know how to write a better report by now." You sound like a parent, because the receiver won't appreciate being talked to like a child.
- Speak for yourself—Don't refer to absent or anonymous people. "A lot of people don't like it when you do…" Let other people speak for themselves. This is a lame move.
- Phrase issues as a statement, not a question. "When are you going to stop dominating the meeting?" As opposed to, "I feel annoyed when you dominate the meeting."
- Don't present your opinions as facts. Just speak the facts. Restrict your feedback to things you know for sure.

You must have good feedback skills—both the giving skills and the receiving skills. Whenever you give any kind of feedback, use these tips.

CHEAT CODES:

Give the feedback as close to the event/behavior as possible—ideally the same day, and in person, if possible. E-mail, phone or text are acceptable options, not the best, but certainly better than nothing.

Pick the right moment. The other person has to be receptive and you have to be well prepared.

Pick the right place. Feedback is best given in private,

even positive feedback. Some people like public compliments and some people hate them. If it's constructive or negative feedback, it must be in private.

You need to give context: where the situation happened, when it happened, what led up to the event or action.

Be specific and objective about what you just saw happen. State just the facts without judgment.

Don't go back in the distant past as a reference to the point you're trying to make—that approach will invite an argument about the facts.

Always, always use "I" statements not "you" statements. Starting with "I" keeps the focus on how you feel versus starting with "You" which sounds like you are accusing the other person.

Tell how the behavior affects you in just one or two words, e.g. disappointed, annoyed, irritated, or angry.

Tell why you felt the way you did and connect the facts to your feelings.

Pause. Let the other person respond.

Then describe the change you like to see. Or have a discussion about possible solutions.

The equation

When you (do this), I feel (this way), because (of such and such). (Pause) What I would like you to consider is (doing X), because I think it will accomplish (Y). What do you think?

Here's an example:

Me: "When I walked into staff meeting this morning, I overheard you telling Melissa a story that I had told you about our boss. I felt disappointed, because I didn't want anyone else to know how I felt. That was meant to be between just me and you."
Pause
You: "Oh well, I had no idea you would have a problem with me telling Melissa."
Me: "I would like you to keep our conversations between us in the future. Can you handle that?"
You: "Yeah if you let me know what you don't want me to share. Thanks for letting me know."

Here's the way to give positive feedback or a full compliment.

CHEAT CODES:

If you want to expand your personal power, you'll give a full compliment.

We were taught to say thank you as kids. Adults need to say more than just thank you, especially if we want to expand our personal power.

Saying "good job" is also the lazy way out. You need

to say specifically what was done well. Include all the specifics of the behavior or act.

Describe why the good behavior or action matters so much to you.

Don't take good behavior for granted.

The more information you give someone about what they did well, the more likely they are to repeat the good behavior.

Here's an example:

Me: "Today I really thought your presentation was totally on point. I thought the charts really supported your topic and your comments were interesting and kept everyone engaged. You spent just the right amount of time. I appreciated that." (Notice how much better this is than "Nice job.")

You: "Thank you." (Now you really liked this gift, didn't you? You now know exactly what you did that I appreciated and you are likely to repeat this performance.)

CHEAT CODES:

Listen carefully. Receive the gift of feedback.

Let the speaker finish all his points. Don't interrupt to defend or ask questions.

When he's done, acknowledge what you heard,

"So you're saying I'm not well-regarded by upper management?"

Ask clarifying questions like, "Can you give me a specific example of what you're talking about?"

If any of the points made were valid, be a big boy/girl and say, "Sometimes I do jump to conclusions too quickly. I see that."

If you are not ready to respond to the feedback, say, "Thank you. I need to think about what you've said. Give me time to think about it and I'll come back to discuss this with you." Take the time to sort out what you heard. The feedback gift may have been delivered in a smelly bag but maybe there's a nugget or two of truth, some good mushrooms, growing in the bag. Try to learn from it. No one is perfect.

Maybe the feedback was totally off base. If that's your perception, then let it go, throw the gift away.

Questions to Consider:

- What do you intend to happen as a result of your feedback?
- Do you give credit where credit is due? Do you do it right after the good thing happens?
- When have you had to give tough feedback to someone?
- What keeps you from giving constructive feedback?
- When you've received constructive feedback, how did you feel?

ADAPTABILITY

There's a lot in this book about all the dramas and bad games that get played out at work. You need to understand the politics at work and you need to be able to respond in the most positive way you can. Frustration and stress are part of the game and you need to learn how to cope. Being capable of adjusting to situations and all kinds of people is a talent—supposedly why humans are the dominant life form on earth. You need to be the grown-up, even when it's the higher-ups that are acting like children.

CHEAT CODES:

Don't react immediately to an uncomfortable situation or someone else's outrageous behavior.

Look for potential benefits in whatever unexpected event has occurred.

Don't buy into the rumor mill.

Hang out with the positive people at work. Surely they exist. Join that fraternity/sorority. Sometimes you need a new peer group. And stay away from the Negative Nellies; they create anxiety you don't need.

Be willing to adapt to other people's working styles— read them and make an adjustment that fits. Maybe the person prefers e-mail versus personal conversation and you need to respect that.

Change your expectations about the work environment. Expect things to be imperfect—messy, stressful, and demanding. This mindset alone will help you roll with the punches.

Humor can help you get through a tough day. Humor can draw people together and lighten a tense situation. Spend time with colleagues who have a good sense of humor.

Decide to see the positive side of things and assume that people have good intentions. Realize that how you view a situation often determines how you approach it.

Avoid personalizing. Most of the things that happen actually aren't aimed at you. You are the one who decides to make it feel like that.

Try to look at the broader context of a bad situation.

When you're under stress, you're likely to react more quickly and intensely. Catch yourself before you say something you might regret. Use self-control. Remember that you can control your emotions. At work, you have to master this skill.

Practice patience. The time may not be right for your idea, but your idea may still be right.

Maybe having a long commute is a good thing—it gives you time to decompress before you get home.

Keep your life in balance. Don't let work dominate your existence. It's not healthy. You will regret it in the end.

Build a strong professional network outside of your organization. These relationships can be a more positive, safe place for you to share your frustrations and concerns.

Identify your stress triggers and get in front of your feelings. Reduce the situations that set off your triggers.

When you find yourself in a trying situation, calm yourself down with deep breathing. Learn to handle stress by exercising, eating well, and relaxing.

Learning to adapt was the biggest skill I mastered. I found that the best way to survive in corporate America was to use my childhood gifts—I watched, listened, adapted, and learned to be in it but not of it, as they say. I stood at a different kind of chain-link fence looking into office environments where people were acting badly at work. I learned that bad behavior and bad decision-making are equal opportunity afflictions—all races, ages, genders, and organizations are susceptible.

Questions to Consider:

- Think of a time in your work life when you had to deal with a big change.
- What emotions did you experience?
- What strategies did you use?
- What was the price of not changing?

MANAGING CONFLICT

If there is more than one person in a situation, there is room for conflict to occur. (It's funny how you can't have conflict by yourself; but you can be "conflicted" which is different.) Conflict is natural and it's not all bad; it can actually be valuable. Good conflict can lead to a breakthrough—to a more creative solution than would have been achieved with groupthink. Groupthink is where everyone is too focused on getting along to allow for honest, healthy debate that would lead to a new perspective. Conflict can create "pearls"—oysters need the irritant of sand to make a pearl.

Just like giving and receiving feedback, managing conflict is a skill many of us didn't learn at home or in school. It takes a lot of skill and practice to manage disagreement well. You have to change your habits and your thinking. Trying to overpower others to accept your position can escalate things at work to attack and protect mode—and that can be a big lose/lose. (See more in the Game Codes section.) If you want to become a master mediator, you've got to start by valuing everyone's opinions, to double check and confirm your understanding of what's causing the conflict.

CHEAT CODES:

You have to have enough credibility to be in the battle.

Get out of the office conference room. Select neutral territory, an informal setting.

Have all the right people present. This is a judgment call. Keep the number of players to a minimum.

All the players need to put on their adult diapers not come to the table wearing their "training pants."

Set an agenda and ground rules. Ground rules are the game parameters: no yelling, no name-calling, no interrupting, no criticizing. Establish whatever guidelines are needed to have a healthy dialogue.

Avoid using highly emotional language or triggers—sarcasm, ignoring, attacking someone's values, inflammatory statements.

Stay open to possibilities.

Have a timekeeper to maintain some discipline. Maybe have a sand timer to limit each debater's speaking time.

Keep active listening and constructive feedback skills high.

If you're the leader or designated facilitator, remain neutral as possible.

Pick on a small element of the conflict to start with that's easy to manage.

Take a break if emotions get too high to let the tension subside.

What I'm saying here is much easier said than done. I know very few people who have these skills. The goal is to increase the positive aspects of conflict and limit the negative aspects—to lead to a good outcome—to get to a compromise, a win/win, or best case, a collaborative solution.

Questions to Consider:

- Have you ever seen a conversation with healthy conflict, not just yelling or crying?
- What was it like?
- What made it work?
- What would you add to the list of conflict management tips?

INTEGRITY

Early in my career, I was in the women's bathroom complaining about my boss with a female colleague who had walked in with me. What I didn't know is that my boss was already in a stall and she heard everything I said. I noticed a difference in her attitude towards me later, but I didn't know why. Later, someone told me that my boss had heard me bitching and she concluded that I was no longer committed to my job. So she had started giving me less challenging assignments. Ouch. At that moment, I knew I had not acted with integrity. I was really stupid for assuming the bathroom was a safe place to bitch and I was stupid for bad-mouthing my boss, period.

CHEAT CODES:

Don't talk behind someone's back.

Be aware that people pay attention to what you do, your attitude, and what you say.

Be consistent. Treat everyone the same.

Live up to your commitments. The equation is: Your Words = Your Actions.

Admit when you are wrong, you apologize, fix it and make amends.

Protect confidential information.

Stand up for what you believe is right, whether you are working with senior leaders, colleagues, and people you work with outside the organization.

Don't let the negative bull people say easily sway you.

Having integrity is the foundation of personal power. If you don't have it, you are totally on the dark side. Most of the Bad Players mentioned have gaps in their integrity.

Questions to Consider:
- Do you keep your promises at work?
- Do you apologize when you've made a mistake?
- Does your quest for success get in the way of your ability to work well with your colleagues?
- Do you know what your values are? Are you faithful to them?
- Did you do your best at work today?

TRUSTWORTHINESS

Trust is the foundation of any relationship. If we don't trust each other, we have no relationship. We have no work team. We're just a collection of individuals working on our own agendas. Without trust, it's really, really hard to get things done with people. Here are some ways that lack of trust play out at work.

- Avoiding you is my top priority. I really don't want to work with you or even speak to you unless absolutely necessary. I don't look forward to meetings that I have to attend with you there.
- I just let you walk around making an ass of yourself. I'm afraid to give you constructive feedback because you'll take it the wrong way.
- I don't tell you anything about my personal life because you will use it against me in some way—to make me look bad or to make you look good by comparison.
- I won't ask you for help, even when I really need it because you will think I am vulnerable and weak. I can't have you thinking that.
- I will not forgive you. You burned me and I will hold a grudge.
- I assume that there is no way your intentions are good.
- I'm just not going to focus on anything positive about you, even if you may be skilled and talented.
- I'll play passive aggressive and pretend to like you in front of the team and the leader.
- I don't ever know what to believe when you speak. So, I tune you out.

- I talk about you behind your back.
- I will sabotage your ass first chance I get.
- I'm just not with you.

To be fair, I believe you should give a new person at work the benefit of the doubt, that is, assume they mean well until they prove otherwise. Watch how a person behaves; observe whether their words and actions match.

Be that person that others trust. (See the section on Good Players—Who Do You Trust?) Trust is the essential ingredient in a working relationship. I'm going to repeat some things I've already said, because I really need to reinforce these powerful points to help you survive in the workplace.

CHEAT CODES:

Focus your time and energy on important issues, not office politics.

Give people the benefit of the doubt before assuming a negative conclusion.

Apologize. Accept apologies.

Be willing to be vulnerable. Admit your weaknesses and ask for help.

Be reliable.

Be consistent.

Do the right things.

Tell the truth.

Don't steal—ideas, attention, or credit—from someone else.

Protect confidentiality.

Show up. Be totally present at work. Do your job and meet expectations.

Look a person in the eye; show open body language. Don't cross your arms, roll your eyes or send other negative body signals.

Seek mutual benefits in your relationships. Don't make it all about you.

Encourage and accept constructive feedback.

Really listen to what others have to say.

Be accountable. Do what you say you are going to do. Set the example.

Focus on solutions, not problems.

Be objective and fair.

While good guys don't always finish first in the short game at work, I guarantee you this approach will pay off for you in the longer game.

Questions to Consider:

- What workplace behaviors do you see that destroy trust?
- How do you react when you don't trust someone at work?
- Do you keep all of your commitments at work?
- Do you look at yourself critically to see how you may have been part of the problem or do you just blame others?
- Why should someone at work trust you?
- Are you always honest or do you play political games for your own gain?

MANAGE YOUR BOSS

No, I'm not talking about kissing the boss's ass or manipulating him. Managing up is a way to get to a win/win situation between you and your manager. You keep him up to speed proactively on projects and issues and he appreciates your initiative. You help him look good; in turn, hopefully, he will return the favor. If you don't manage your relationship with your boss, you risk getting overlooked for career opportunities—you could become invisible. It's all about communication and initiative.

When I was a manager, I loved my employees who took initiative with me. They were the ones I knew I could count on to take care of problems without needing me to get involved. They built strong trust with me and I was able to delegate greater responsibility to them, so they could grow into new, higher roles. I also loved that my employees who were good at managing up, came to me with multiple alternatives to a problem or issue.

Another reason to manage your boss is so you can get work done with minimal interference. The more your boss trusts you, the less he will micromanage you. By managing up, you buy yourself more independence and space to do your work. You almost become your own boss.

How do you manage your boss? First, do a good analysis and diagnosis of who you are dealing with—to understand his needs and wants and how he operates. Then you need to understand your own strengths and weaknesses and how to use your strengths to support and compliment your manager. When you master this game, you will get more of your ideas pushed through your boss and on up to higher management. The game of managing up that I'm talking about here is a game of integrity, not ego, and it is a critical game to master, especially if you want to grow into higher responsibility and get promoted. It's about being proactive, assertive, and strategic. This is what grown-ups do at work.

When you're good at this game, you help your boss to help you. First of all, you need to earn your manager's trust.

CHEAT CODES:

Show that you are committed to the goals of the department and the organization overall, not just to getting ahead.

Be the kind of employee who not only delivers great work but who understands how to work well with others.

Be proactive. Anticipate the needs of your boss to make his life easier. (Again, this is not brown-nosing or playing politics if done with integrity and the right intention, which is to be helpful.)

Take initiative. Don't wait to be told what to do next.

Offer suggestions that benefit the entire team or effort.

Negotiate on deadlines if you need to when you face competing priorities. Clarify with your boss so you can get the right things done in the timeframe. You are not challenging the priorities; you just want to understand the parameters better.

Be a problem-solver, not a problem-bringer. Every boss appreciates an employee who comes in with a problem and some proposed solutions.

Questions to Ask Your Boss

(Also great interview questions!)
1. How would you describe your management/leadership style?
2. What is your definition of a top performer?
3. How do you prefer that I communicate with you?
4. What does success for our team look like to you?
5. What are the biggest challenges you face in your role?
6. What are your expectations of me?

OFFICE GAMING STRATEGIES

So you've read about all the games and players. Now what? It's all about survival of the fittest. Here are some more strategies for dealing with specific games and players, to add on to the ones already presented. These are more Cheat Codes or countermoves—actions you need to take to break the pattern of a game and get the focus back on the work.

Backstabber: If someone has a knife in your back, take it out, hand it to him and let him know you don't play that—you won't let him stab you. Right then and there. Don't put up with anybody trying to tear you down. It's a power game. First, you need to make sure you have your facts straight—is he really stabbing you in the back or is this a misunderstanding? Then you rehearse and prepare what you're going to say. Be calm. Don't just go at him while you're all heated up about his behavior.

Ball Hog: Be the one to take this person aside and have a little chat about sharing. Maybe he doesn't realize he's being greedy with his time demands. Remember, feedback is a gift and he needs you to show him a mirror. Now the risk is, he knows good and well what he's doing and is on ego-overdrive so he will turn on you. You make the call.

Cut-Down: Stay strong and don't let his put-downs get to you. Never let him see you sweat or lose your self-confidence—he wants to hurt you and drag you down. Ignore him and stay away from this chronic complainer—he usually has no political power anyway—he's just annoying to be around. Find some positive people to hang around. If you're worried that the criticism is real, check it out with someone you trust, who is not an emotional midget.

Gossiper: Ignore the rumors you hear. You don't need anything more than is necessary taking up time and space in your workday. When you do confront someone who has been gossiping, focus on the issue and behavior rather than on the person. For example, instead of saying, "You are a bad person for gossiping about me," say instead, "I am concerned about the gossiping, and I want it to stop." Don't get drawn in—when you hear people talking about someone who is absent, stay out of the conversation or try to change the subject. Don't get all self-righteous about it—just be subtle and firm. They'll get the message.

Hater: Ignore him. Try not to let him see that his evilness is getting to you. Hater's gonna hate. Don't try to work things out with him. You can't make everyone happy. Everyone doesn't deserve your time or friendship. Don't give them power over you by letting them make you feel bad.

Hypercritic: If this character is your boss, you need to be in control. You need to please him, unfortunately, if you want to keep your job and get ahead with the company. Try to talk to him to clarify what it is exactly that he expects from you and how you can get ahead of the curve. Get used to not getting a lot of praise—he's just not one who focuses on the positive. It doesn't mean you're not deserving of recognition, you're just going to have to get it from somewhere else—inside yourself, peers or others at work. When he goes off on you, just let it roll off your back. If this character is a peer, who cares what he has to say? Tell him to back off and mind his own business. (See section on Micromanagers, as well.)

Idea Harassment: This is going to happen and you need to get used to it. Sorry. It's a fact of corporate life that everyone wants to contribute their goodness to your idea, especially the higher ups. So take your ego down a few notches. It's not personal. It's not a lack of trust. You may not like what becomes of your original concept. Let it go. Someday, when you're running the shop, maybe you can see your ideas through all the way without any meddling. And maybe, just maybe, the meddlers are not harassing your idea but making it better.

Imposter: If you're brave enough, out him for the phony that he is. Don't let him get away with getting shine for the wrong reason when he doesn't have the goods. Or you can just ignore him but keep your eye on his sneaky activities.

Invisible Work Horse: Take off your invisibility cloak, Harry Potter. Toot your horn, brag about your accomplishments, ask to be included in meetings, ask for new assignments. Step it up and let your voice be heard. Often good guys finish last in the office games.

Kissin' Ass: Encourage the ass kissers (you'll recognize when their tongues are out with management) to be more candid in discussions at meetings. You want to out them in the meeting, but not in a way that makes them look bad. Steer the discussion to the facts on the table, versus allowing any personal agenda to be the focus.

Late Dog: Gotta give him some feedback, man. Assume he doesn't realize the negative impact he is having on the team. You can say, "Hey, we really can't get into the real issues without you, so try to be on time." Or, "I feel like you don't care about how important the meeting is when you come in late. I need you to be on time to show the team you respect our time."

Narcissist (Bad Ones): This is a tough one. You can't change this person. You can't argue with them. He thinks, no, he knows that he knows everything. The narcissist only knows one game: "I win." In fact, there's only one player in this equation, really. You can choose to give him what he wants which is lots of praise, even for the tiniest thing and no criticism or at least not without lots of sugarcoating it. Never disagree or contradict him. Don't make any comment that might offend his ego in any way (his image of perfection defines his self-worth). Don't waste your time trying to bring him into reality or seeing an alternative rationale—as the rest of the world would view it. You might even try kissing his ass if you feel so inclined—he would love that! Other Narcissistic players include some Ball Hogs, Gossipers, and Haters.

Passive Aggression: Be the one person who calls this nonsense out. I hate this game of not being direct. Say things like, "Just tell me what you really want me to do. Stop beating around the bush." Or, "Give it to me straight." Or, "I don't think you're saying what you really mean. I can take it."

Power Games: Stand your ground. If someone is challenging you, set him straight right away. Establish your position, hold firm, and keep the discussion about the work. Don't get drawn into an adversarial game by being vengeful—that brings you right to the level this player wants. If you get emotionally hooked into this game, it could become destructive. Try using resistance—when someone is pushing you, don't push back, don't give in, and don't argue. Instead say something like, "You make an interesting point. I'll keep that in mind."

Predator: Avoid him but watch him—he has no good intentions. He's usually pretty overt in this negative behavior toward you. Stand up to him. Protect yourself as best you can. Document the predatory behavior if you can. Get some witnesses. Get your work posse on your side.

Scapegoat/Blamer: If you are the target of blame, deflect attention from yourself by getting the facts on the table that support your case. Don't get defensive or emotional and don't argue about the issue. You need to broaden beyond yourself to the thing that happened. If it's your boss who's playing this game, you may have to go with the CYA strategy (cover your ass).

Sink or Swim: Ask for help. Make some friends fast—the people who know what's up. Surely someone in the place can show you the ropes. Stay late and work extra to learn and catch up. This is especially challenging when you are newly promoted—not only do you not know how to lead or manage, but also you have to learn the new assignment. Ouch! Take the initiative in finding a training class or seminar and ask your manager to let you attend—on the company's dime of course. Try not to run to your boss every five minutes with questions—ask someone else.

Snake: Harder to watch this character because he is very sneaky and passive aggressive. Don't fall for the smile in your face—you may get bit as soon as you are comfortable. Don't trust him. Tune in to your intuition.

Snubbing: Best move here is to divide and conquer this group of bullies. One of them is sure to be less invested in being as mean as the others. Develop a relationship with the weakest players—that should help you short circuit the game.

Sorority/Fraternity: Somehow you've got to get these groups to include you. Bring the issue up straight. Say, "Sometimes decisions are getting made between you guys before I can weigh in. What's up with that?" Or try to find an individual in the group that you can build a relationship with, sincerely. It's too hard to take on the whole group clique or department.

Squawking: When this disruptive bird comes flying into your team project, it's best if you can get the whole team to sit down with him collectively and explain that his approach is messing with your flow. He needs to understand that while he may think he's being helpful, he's really making things harder. If he only does it to you individually, the message is the same—he's leaving poop piles in his wake and it's taking you off task to clean them up. Don't treat him as a predator; his intentions are honorable.

Suggestion Jerk-Off: If your boss steals your ideas or puts them on a back burner, just refuse to provide suggestions unless you are empowered to act on them. Save them for a better time, a more receptive audience.

Superstar: I personally want to know this person, not to kiss up to them, but to learn how they succeeded in getting all the shine. Don't get too close to them because the haters will come after both of you. And keep in mind the stardom is always temporary. Don't be jealous.

Supremacy: Try to be sympathetic by remembering that these players are actually insecure beneath all their swag. Ignore their self-promoting, bragging comments. If you don't reward their annoying behavior, hopefully they will get the message. Never try to play one-up with these players because it will just start a cycle—a tennis match—between the two of you competing for biggest size prize.

Work Avoidance Technician: You may be tempted to go right at this slacker, but that will just make him procrastinate even more. Always get the slippery player to commit to specific dates in writing—e-mail will work—even if you feel certain he will not make the date. Smart move here is to pad the due date because you know this unreliable player will screw up your timeline if you don't. Sometimes you may want to copy this player's boss on that e-mail, just to raise the level of seriousness. Maybe when he sees that his manager has been copied, he'll step up. If work avoider is your boss, then this won't work.

For all the other bad players, the strategy is simple. Avoid or ignore them as best you can. For the other sad players you can have sympathy for them but you just have to ignore them; they have to learn to stand up for themselves.

Step Up To The Plate – Be a Good Lifetime Player

STEP UP TO THE PLATE—BE A GOOD LIFETIME PLAYER

If you learn how to walk in the minefield of work, I'm hoping you will be less likely to plant the landmines to trap others. I'm counting on you to make the workplace function better. Maybe people won't want to change jobs as often. Maybe employers will enjoy less frequent turnover. I'm counting on you to change the world of work. We need more civility at work. We need good players at work. We need good leaders. I'm counting on you. Speak your truth, be a role model for the good, and be ready to handle the backlash from the bad players.

"Your work is going to fill a large part of your life, and the only way to be truly satisfied is to do what you believe is great work. And the only way to do great work is to love what you do. If you haven't found it yet, keep looking. Don't settle. As with all matters of the heart, you will know it when you find it." Steve Jobs

I've given you the benefit of my knowledge and experience. You need to take these tips and apply them. I hope you can recognize more of the pitfalls and learn how to cope.

Make a good choice.
You need to decide what you want out of your job:
- What fits with your passion?
- What showcases your talents?
- What kind of people do you want to work with?
- What kind of leader will motivate you best?

- What does the ideal work environment look like to you?
- How much are you willing to give?
- What are you willing to tolerate?

I realize that sometimes you just have to get a J-O-B. If you're just graduating from college you can't expect to get the ideal job. You just need to get started in life and pay back your student loans. This may lead you on a path that you don't want to be on, but if you keep your eye on the bigger prize, you will learn something, regardless. If you have a family to feed, you can't just walk away from your bi-monthly paycheck and benefits. You can sell your soul to the devil and stay or you keep your nose to the grindstone until you can find a way to get on a better road. Sometimes the have to overrides the want to. Don't lose sight of who you really are and what you really want out of life. Ever.

May the Force be with you!

The Force, if you choose to believe, is an energy field that can be used by individuals who are sensitive to it. It is in everyone. It is your personal power. Use of the Force can give you the ability to sense impending attacks at work, influence others and protect you from the toxic workplace.

Put on your invisible armor.

Go into work with a force field of positive energy around you. You can imagine it like a gigantic protective bubble that keeps you separated from the bad energy, bad players, and general negativity you may face. How you spend your days—what you think about and pursue—directly affects your future (for better or worse). You want to invest your time and energy into the things and people you're passionate about, and the dreams you have, rather than soaking up the negative energy like Sponge Bob, the cartoon character. Letting bad people twist you around gives them power and takes power from you. Don't give them your power. Don't let the craziness that happens at work bring hate and fear into your life. You need to let it go. Remember: This too shall pass.

Don't take it personally.

Do not let things that happen at work get inside your soul. Practice being in it and not of it. When something happens that rubs you the wrong way at work—a nasty e-mail, a bad decision—notice it, acknowledge how you feel about it and then put a checkmark on a sticky note that you keep on your desk to give yourself points for ignoring it, not reacting. If you lose your cool or fall for the bad player, you lose a point on your sticky note.

The only person you can change is you.

Don't think for one minute that you will have so much influence over someone at work that you can make that person better. The only person you can change is you. So work on making yourself better.

"If you don't like something, change it. If you can't change it, change your attitude." Maya Angelou

Find the humor.

It's so easy to get broke down at work. You're overwhelmed by the amount of work, the long hours, the people getting on your nerves. It's natural to freak out when the going gets tough. I encourage you to find humor in the situation, however you can. Humor will keep your spirit up.

A brand called "You."

Everyone is walking around as an advertisement for who he or she is. Define your brand, live it, protect it. Be mindful of your behavior and your performance at work because what you do is your brand, your reputation. So what is your personal VMV—vision, mission and values—statement? If you're not branding yourself, you can be sure others will do it for you.

"Brand yourself for the career you want, not the job you have." – Dan Schawbel, author and workplace expert

Find good mentors.

When you find a trusted advisor, sit at their feet and learn. Let someone help you get through your workplace issues. You can't do this alone. There are good people out there. Don't be an idiot and think you know all the games and how to play—you don't and you can't. This psychological crap is hard and complex. I was fortunate to have good role models and mentors along the way who helped me hold it together. God bless them one and all.

"A mentor is someone who allows you to see the hope inside yourself." — Oprah Winfrey

Take time to do what makes your soul happy.

You have to train your mind, body, and spirit for the workplace battle, just like a professional actor, singer, or athlete. Get in the zone. Balance is the key. If you let work dominate your life, you will become dull—in every way.

Consider taking yoga—not to stand on your head—but to learn how to breathe. Breathing is a great way to center yourself and not be in the issue or the emotion of a situation. Your breath is always accessible to you as a tool. Being able to calm your nervous system and your brain will help you survive the frustration and insanity. You have to take care of yourself first. Boxing is another mindfulness and awareness activity. It will heighten your focus, your perspective. You become exquisitely alert after a workout and it carries on for hours. It's a great way to work out the frustration, anxiety, and anger you may feel after a bad day at work.

Use your PTO for mental health days.

I don't mean for you to take a vacation day. Stay home and focus on your self. Be selfish. Don't think about work. Focus on you. This is especially important when you feel beat down by the work or the people you work with. This is to keep you from killing someone or killing yourself.

When I worked at corporate, I would choose to work from home as often as allowed. Even working from home was health giving—I was actually much more productive and happier working from home. Ultimately, I realized this was my destiny, to work from home, and so I hung a shingle and became an independent consultant. I'm happier even though I make less money than I would have if I'd stayed on the corporate ladder. And for me, no doubt, my mental state is much better.

Get some perspective.

Read about things that really matter, beyond work. Find books that speak to your soul, entertain you, or build your knowledge and skill of human dynamics. You have to work with people so the more you understand about the psychology of the human race, the better off you will be. (See the list of resources at the end of the book.)

Part 2:
Real-Life Stories:
Games People Play

PART 2: REAL-LIFE STORIES: GAMES PEOPLE PLAY

Most of these stories came from people in my network—colleagues and friends—and some from my own experiences. I can't even remember the source of each story. The names and organizations are fake. I can assure you that my intention is to teach, not to "out" anyone, to cause harm, or to be vindictive.

In the end, reflecting back on some of these situations and putting a smile on your face will help you realize there is nothing wrong with you. Or that there is something wrong with you but you're not alone! Or that people are crazier than you could have ever realized. Or at least, I hope you have your eyes open and understand what you are seeing. Then you can make an intentional choice about how to react.

I'm sure you'll see situations you can relate to. While the work experiences may vary, the same corporate politics and human dynamics exist whether you work in the Northeast, Midwest, West Coast, or internationally, and whether you work for a nonprofit, in the private sector, government, or any type of institution. Where there's more than one person at work besides you, there's room for issues.

Leadershit

When Nolan joined the company as head of talent and organization development, he spent the first two weeks interviewing managers in all the functions to understand how they felt about his department. He didn't spend any one-on-one time with his dozen staff members during those first two weeks. Week three, Nolan called his first staff meeting with the recruiters and HR specialists after gathering the cross-functional input.

Nolan: "Does anyone have any questions before we address the agenda at hand?"

Morgan, one of the recruiters who was an introvert, raised her hand, Gina looked at her, jokingly and said, "Huh, I didn't even know you could talk. Ha!" Morgan was so offended that she didn't bother to ask her question.

Welcome to the first meeting with the new boss.

Nolan proceeds to tell everyone: "You all are making my job harder. During my cross-functional fact gathering, I heard that all of you are well liked. I was hoping to get consistent feedback that at least three of you three needed to be fired. Ha!"

No one laughed.

Nolan: "I'm planning to do a reorg in three weeks. I'll come back and let you know who has a job."

Keep in mind; Nolan said this after just a few weeks on the job and without meeting with any of the team members individually. After the meeting, each person started jockeying to keep his job—to save his own ass with the new boss. All previous teamwork fell to the wayside. Nolan played mind games, pitting individuals against one other and letting each one know how he could get on his good side.

Coda: The mind games here are advanced level power abuse. The competitors chose to play though, so that's their bad.

Demoted

Parker and Janice were both project directors on software rollouts. They were strong performers and they both had been promoted about a year ago. They were the only two people in the department at their level, and each of them had three to four project managers reporting to them.

Willie was hired as the new head of the department. His first decision was to flatten the organization chart—to have less hierarchy. Without evaluating Parker's or Janice's performance records or even meeting with them, Willie decided to eliminate the title of project director. Willie sent an e-mail to Janice and to Parker the evening of his very first day on the job. The e-mail said:

"Effectively immediately you are being demoted to project manager. All project managers will report to me. Your salary will remain the same. Since you are no longer in the Director category of the bonus pool, you will not participate in the company bonus program."

Janice and Parker were shocked and upset by this decision, of course. Not only were they losing their status, but also it was hitting their paychecks. And the fact that they had to learn this in an e-mail was really messed up. Willie stopped by their shared office first thing in the morning, very cheery.

Willie: "Morning guys! Did you have any questions about my e-mail?"

Neither one of them responded. Within a month, Parker left for a better job. Janice followed suit the following month. Willie didn't care.

Coda: This is one of the worst uses of e-mail I have ever seen. Terrible leadership.

Highly Paid Babysitter

Chase was hired to lead the sales team of ten people at a toy company. He was a former colleague of the operations manager, Tony, so he was hired on Tony's recommendation. The traditional interview process was bypassed (which should have been the first red flag). Normally, Chase would have been interviewed by some of the sales staff, as well as HR.

Within the first thirty days, all of the sales staff knew that Chase was going to be a problem. Chase was spending more time traveling and entertaining clients than leading the sales strategy and guiding the team. When the team asked for insights/feedback related to customers, products, or to help resolve issues, Chase had nothing to contribute. He would say, "I'm sure you can figure it out." Or if he did weigh in, he made bad decisions that created chaos in the organization and negatively impacted customers. The team then became nothing more than cleaners—fixing all the messes Chase was making.

When Chase did interact with his sales team, he was only interested in monitoring their whereabouts. He had to know where each of the ten salespeople were at all times—nine of them were scattered all over the U.S., where Chase couldn't see them on a daily basis.

A meeting was scheduled at the corporate office and all of the salespeople were coming in from out of town, arriving at different times. Chase asked them to provide detailed itineraries. The one salesperson based at corporate, Marcy picked up one of her peers,

Javier, at the airport. On the way to Javier's hotel, he checked his mobile and saw six text messages from Chase. Then his cell phone rang. It was Chase.

Chase: "I was trying to reach you, why didn't you return my call?"

Javier: "I was on the plane and had my phone in airplane mode. You had my itinerary. I thought you knew that I'd be out of touch while I was on the plane."

Chase: "Oh, you should have called me back anyway. Where are you now?"

Marcy and Javier just looked at each other and rolled their eyes. This man was a lunatic.

Coda: If you're really smart, you'll learn to anticipate the minutia-level game and give this person as much insignificant, unnecessary detail as you can to keep them off your case.

The Vision Statement is a Joke

Lucas was the head of product development for a company that designed office accessories. The company vision statement was "To become the most innovative producer of office accessories in the world"—a pretty audacious goal.

In reality, Lucas's team of designers watched the product leaders in the market and quickly "followed" with similar prototypes (copies). Lucas was a very talented industrial designer. His designs won industry awards. Several of the young designers who worked for Lucas were not happy with the "design copying" strategy that the company followed and wanted to branch out and do original designs. Lucas was a very nice person and didn't want to have anyone on his team unhappy. So he allowed the complainers to go beyond the boundaries and do new designs. The problem was the company didn't want to spend the money to get proprietary patents for unique designs because of the expense. Lucas knew this was the strategy, but he allowed those designers to work on innovation.

When one of the designers presented his creative concepts to the management team, the CEO shut him down. Lucas was too intimidated to stand up to the leaders and support his team member's innovative work. That particular team member quit. The remaining designers were disgruntled because Lucas kept them inside the box. The design team lost productivity. Lucas found he had to work more hours to make up for the lack of productivity from his designers.

Coda: *The management team wasn't drinking their own Kool-Aid. The reality is, when you see a disconnect between the talk and the walk, you probably need to leave and go someplace where these two things are aligned.*

I'm Not Your Negro

Vickie, a newly hired, white female manager, was talking to one of her direct reports, Rhonda, an African American female, for the first time. Vickie had let it be known that she highly valued loyalty from her team.

Vickie: "Girlfriend, at my last company, one of my best employees was African American. She always kept me in the loop and I did the same for her. So you can do that for me."

Rhonda thought (but didn't say this): "I may be the only brown person here but I'm not going to kiss your ass. And we are not friends. You just started here so don't assume I'm going to be your mole, bitch."

Coda: Is every African American female automatically going to be your girlfriend at work, just because one was? Don't assume that all the sisters are going to be cool with you.

Back Off

Sophie worked for a company that imported products from India. At times, the CEO, Jackson, would travel overseas by himself to visit factories. Sophie dreaded these visits. She would get phone calls at two in the morning from Jackson while he was in a factory asking a question about a project. She'd come into the office in the morning and read through numerous e-mails from Jackson that described all the changes he had made to products, packaging, colors, etc., while he was in the factory. Sophie couldn't figure out why Jackson felt compelled to become involved in projects when he had no idea about what was going on. It would be like having a dentist perform open-heart surgery.

Coda: The two players here need a serious sit down conversation about roles, responsibilities and process change.

Female Rivalry

Cassie and Benita were peers on a very high performing team—all women. They all got along well and were very productive in their region. The national leader decided to promote Cassie to be the director of our group so that he would have fewer direct reports. With her new position, Cassie's behavior towards the team changed dramatically. She terrorized one of our team members, Martina, an African American woman, to the point that Martina was actually afraid that Cassie would assault her. Sadly, Martina quit.

Then Benita, a Guatemalan female, became Cassie's next victim. She started asking Benita to give a detailed account of all of her time and got very nit-picky about her work products. Benita had no idea why she became the target of Cassie's wrath. Remember, prior to Cassie's promotion, this was a very high performing team. Benita had played a major role in that performance as she had been on the team longer than anyone. Cassie's intimidation of Benita was unfair and unwarranted. She didn't ask other team members to do the things she was asking of Benita. At one point, Cassie wrote a negative e-mail about Benita's performance to her boss and accidentally copied Benita on it. So then Benita knew for a fact that she was being documented. Cassie was really out to get rid of her.

Benita finally went to employee relations to complain and file a formal grievance against Cassie. Someone must have talked to Cassie because suddenly, she changed her tune and starting treating Benita with respect.

Later, Benita found out that she and Martina had been hired in at a higher pay grade than Cassie (they had more experience). With Cassie's promotion, she was still not at their pay level, which was a limitation of the organization's compensation policy. Once Cassie became the director, she had access to that information and Martina and Benita became her targets. The saddest part is that the region never achieved its former performance level under Cassie's direction. None of the remaining team members could understand why Cassie would purposely destroy a very successful operation.

Coda: Going to HR is the right thing to do when someone is targeting you and you feel harassed. You can only hope that: 1) you have an HR department to go to, 2) HR will do the right thing and 3) the offender will get chastised accordingly. Unfortunately, HR doesn't always do the right thing—life isn't always fair. Then you just pray to the universe for karma.

M.F.

Asher hired a new project manager, Phillip, to work in a satellite construction office in another state. Asher had not met him in person, but the salesman in that region, Jordan, had recommended him. So Asher took a chance and hired Phillip after a phone interview. Phillip flew to headquarters for a week to get training on specialized equipment installs for a week. Asher asked another new project manager, Clare, to pick Phillip up from the airport and to take him straight to a construction site to meet Asher and immediately begin training for the two of them. When Phillip arrived, he insisted that Clare take him to his hotel so he could shower. Clare reminded Phillip that the plan, which he knew about, was to go straight to the site for training once he landed, but she reluctantly took him to his hotel. Clare texted Asher while she waited in her car. A short time later, Phillip called Clare.

Phillip: "Hey Clare, come up to Room 430. You've got to check out all the mirrors in my room."

Clare: "Uh, no thanks. I've seen mirrors before. You need to hurry up man, we're running really late."

Phillip: "Aw come on, don't be so uptight."

Clare stayed in her car, very annoyed. Did he think she was stupid enough to go into a hotel room with a guy she didn't even know?

She was not looking forward to spending a whole week with this character.

When they arrived at the worksite for training, over an hour late, Clare was very apologetic to Asher about the delay, but Phillip was not. Asher was surprised at the cocky, easily distracted attitude Phillip presented. Within moments of his arrival, he told Asher that he was going out to dinner with a salesman from his region, Jordan, who happened to be at headquarters for a meeting. Asher thought, "I'm meeting this dude for the first time and that's the first thing he has to say to me?" During the onsite training, Phillip showed glaring unfamiliarity with common install practices that he had claimed to already have in his knowledge base. He was not listening or focusing. He bad-mouthed the way they were doing the project and was pretty disrespectful to Asher, his new boss. At this point, Asher texted his boss: "This guy Phillip is a cowboy."

On day two, Asher met Clare and Phillip at a recently completed restaurant project site so they could see the equipment in use, in real time. The restaurant was actually open for business, buzzing with customers. Asher left Clare and Phillip there to walk around on their own to observe and headed off to an emergency at another worksite. When Asher got back to the office, he received a call from the owner at the restaurant that Clare and Phillip had visited. The owner was livid.

Restaurant Owner: "Someone name Phillip was just in here this afternoon. He was criticizing our staff and acting like he owned the place. He had the nerve to hit on our female bartender. He was relentless with her. His behavior was ridiculous. I never want him in our restaurant again! There was a young lady with him who was trying to reel him in. We all felt sorry for her."

Asher called a meeting with his boss and HR. All agreed that Phillip had to go.

Asher called Clare: "Clare, we're going to fire Phillip. I'm sorry you had to deal with him for the past two days. Listen, if you ever to have another experience like the hotel request, you should take a harder line. Don't ever feel you have to tolerate anything bordering on sexual harassment."

Asher's boss also called Clare to apologize and thank her. The next day, with Phillip safely on a plane and emotions settled, they all met and debriefed again. Asher's boss told him that he had received an e-mail from their biggest competitor in that region that said, "Congratulations on your new hire and good luck!" Funny how the word had traveled fast in the industry that they had hired Phillip.

Coda: Mental illness? Drug addiction? Bat-shit crazy? Let's just say there are a lot of people at work posing as normal. It is a very small world—I'll bet Phillip's former employer was hoping he'd poison their competitor.

Venom

Liz and Bryson started at the company the same day in the same department. They became friends, hanging out on the weekends with their respective partners. When their boss left the company, Liz came up with an idea to present to management.

Liz: "Hey let's go to management and suggest that rather than filling the director's job, they make us co-directors—you can handle the international market, I'll handle domestic."

Bryson thought this was a great idea. Since he was more of an introvert, he was glad that Liz offered to take the proposal forward. A couple of weeks later, an e-mail went out announcing that Liz was being promoted to director; she was now Bryson's boss. Hmmm. Bryson wondered how that happened. He was suspicious that Liz had manipulated her way into the role, but he couldn't prove it. So Bryson just kept doing his job, his relationship with Liz began to change, now that she was in the power seat.

A few weeks later, Liz got very sick and fainted while talking to Bryson in her office. Bryson managed to pick her up and in the process, Liz peed all over him. (This is common when someone loses it.) She regained consciousness and was very embarrassed. Bryson discreetly helped her to his car and took her to see his doctor, who was also a personal friend. The doctor examined Liz, gave her some medication, and Bryson took her home. Liz was very grateful that she had been saved the further embarrassment of being wheeled away on a gurney in front of everyone—which is what would have happened if Bryson had just called 911.

Bryson continued to do his job working, enjoying the work with business partners in Southeast Asia. The Asian partners liked him so much that they called the president of the company stateside and asked that Asher be assigned exclusively to their market. And they told Asher. When Asher was back to the U.S., he went to see the president. He was so excited about getting this new assignment. The president said that he had to discuss it with Liz, however, since she was his boss. Bryson was sure that Liz would be supportive. This move was a no brainer— or so he thought.

Liz: "Well you can't have the assignment overseas. We need you too much here. In fact, I'm going to reassign you to the domestic market exclusively."

Damn. Asher couldn't believe Liz could do him like that. He was pissed. What a bitch! By then, he knew he was done with Liz and the company. He had saved her ass, she had peed all over him and now she was totally dissin' him. Asher left the company and started his own business. He became very successful—the best revenge of all.

Coda: You've got to figure out who to trust and who not to trust fast.

Domination

You are by far the most productive and innovative person on your small sales team. You've handled the workload when your immediate boss was away on a sabbatical, without dropping any balls. You handled all the accounts—the work of two people—without complaint. Your department's revenues and profits have been growing steadily since you came on the team almost three years ago. You've been trusted to make your own decisions on this million-dollar business. You've endured several leadership changes and never lost your drive. Last month, a new guy was moved into your department, two levels above you, named Karl. Karl was from the U.K. and has been with the company many years, but this is his first assignment in the U.S. and his first assignment in product development.

Karl's style is to manage and control every detail. You can no longer make any decisions. In fact, your immediate boss can't make any decisions either. Karl wants to control all thoughts, ideas, and actions. He makes no effort to learn from you or anyone else. Karl spends a lot of time kissing the ass of his new boss, as well. The whole team environment has changed. What do you do? You start losing your "MO-JO"—your commitment and drive.

Coda: I'm thinking that Karl had a very big ego and perhaps some big insecurities as well.

A Cluster

Zara had an idea about celebrating the 100th anniversary of the brand based on her consumer insight research. She told her boss, Emilio, who thought it was an awesome idea. Emilio presented the idea to his boss, Jay, who then put his own spin on the idea, diluting its power. Then the next level boss put his spin on it. By the time the anniversary celebration plan got back to Zara, it was nothing like the original idea she had floated. The worst part about this was that none of the people who impacted the plan had the benefit of the consumer insights that Zara had. Their changes were purely based on their own intuition and/or misinformation. She was not proud to have to execute the watered down, lame brand-anniversary plan.

Coda: You've got to keep the faith, even when your ideas get diluted. Don't take it personally when the boss and his boss put their goodness in your soup pot.

Too Close

The company just hired a new VP of Marketing, Abigail. Within two weeks, Abigail brought in Charles, an employee who had worked for Abigail at her last company. The other seven members of the marketing team picked up right away that Charles was close to Abigail. Every morning, Charles would spend time in Abigail's office drinking coffee and then come back to the rest of the team and tell them "his version of what Abigail said." As the work progressed, he would tell her teammates, "Oh that's not how Abigail would want that done." Some of the staff began to wonder if Abigail and Charles were lovers. Eventually, the top performer on the team left the group because he just couldn't stand Charles or Abigail. The leader, Abigail, was somehow oblivious to the whole situation.

Coda: You have to keep appropriate distance in the workplace, no matter how close you may feel to an employee personally. As the boss, you don't get to play favorites.

Fire Me, Please

Robert came to work late every day and he smelled like alcohol. He sat at his desk and seemed to be working. He left everyday just a little too shy of quitting time. Everyone around him knew he wasn't doing a damn thing, but no one said anything. They all knew that Robert had been through a nasty divorce and felt he deserved some slack. One day, Robert didn't come in and he didn't call in. He didn't answer his phone when his supervisor called his house. He didn't come in the next day either. His supervisor finally reached Robert on Day Three of not showing up.

Supervisor: "Hey Robert, I don't know what's going on with you dude, but you haven't answered my calls. If you don't come in today, you're fired."

Robert: "Whatever."

When the supervisor cleaned out Robert's desk, he found several months of customer invoices that weren't sent out. There were no personal items in his desk at all. The reality is, Robert had actually been "checked out" for months and because everyone was tippy-toeing around him, they didn't realize just how bad it was. It was a hot mess. All that cash from unissued invoices just sitting in a drawer.

Coda: *Leaders, put on your big boy pants and get rid of bad performers promptly. Otherwise you will lose points with the rest of the employees.*

Behind the back Boss

Harper was the Chief Financial Officer (CFO) of a bank. She had been in this position for five years and was considered a strong member of the executive team by her peers. A new Chief Executive Officer (CEO), David, was hired when the previous leader retired. Harper felt she had a good working relationship with David, though not as good as the relationship she had with the previous CEO. She felt very confident in her role and worked very hard to keep the bank's strong financial ratings. In fact, under her leadership, the bank always passed its annual audit with an "A+" rating.

Harper started to notice that David was taking little potshots at her and her team, mostly behind her back, but sometimes even in meetings when she was present. Over time, David's snide remarks and critiques of the finance department became more and more unpleasant for Harper. So she confronted David.

Harper: "Hey David, seems like you're having a problem with me and my team. Is there something we need to discuss?"

David: "What? I don't know what you're talking about, Harper."

Harper: "Well let me show you a few e-mails I've printed out from you to me and to my team members. Seems pretty clear to me that you're not happy about our work."

David: "I think you've over-reacting. I don't think these e-mails are inflammatory at all. If anything, my concern is that you are too sensitive."

Harper: "So we're good? There's nothing wrong with my performance or the performance of my team?"

David: "Yeah, we're good."

A few weeks later, Harper got a letter on her desk stating that she'd been fired effectively immediately. There was no explanation except, "Your services are no longer needed." She was shocked, pissed, hurt, and angry as hell. David refused to talk to her. One of the HR managers came to her office, told her to pack up her personal belongings, and escorted Harper out of the building. Just like that. Harper was embarrassed as she walked past her peers on the way to the elevator.

David underestimated Harper, however. She marched right out and got an employment attorney and threatened to sue David and the bank. She didn't get her job back—and she didn't want it back—but she got two year's salary as compensation. And she didn't have to deal with David's passive aggression anymore.

***Coda:** Smart move here player—saving those e-mails and texts—the good ones and the bad ones. You never know when this strategy will come in handy in a severance negotiation or legal action.*

The Christmas Card

Danita was the administrative support for two different work teams. Team A treated Danita well and always included her in their meetings and social events. Team B didn't include her in their important meetings, leaving Danita in the dark about priorities and deadlines. For Christmas, she got a card from Team B with a picture of everyone on the team, including an outside consultant, excluding Danita. Really? The picture was taken at Team B's leader's home at an event that Danita was obviously excluded from. Not cool.

Coda: Danita couldn't afford to quit her job so she just endured.

Culpability

Anthony was hired as the Chief People Officer (CPO) for a mid-sized company. His resume was stellar and the president of the company, Connor, was delighted to have someone with his experience on board. The prior CPO had not done the job well, so Connor was excited to have Anthony come in and turn things around. Anthony started out well—he got a new HR system installed and hired several new HR managers to support the business.

One day, an employee, Luca, went to see Anthony because his paystub showed that Luca had earned no vacation days, when in fact, he knew he had fifteen days of vacation unused for the year. Anthony told Luca that he would look into it. A few days later, two more employees came in with the same concern. Apparently, the new HR system had zeroed out everyone's vacation days. Now this seems like a simple problem to remedy, right? Well it wasn't simple and Anthony couldn't figure out how to fix the system. So

Anthony announced that no one would be allowed to take any vacation days off until the problem could be fixed. The employees were not happy about this, to say the least. People had plans with their families, trips already paid for, and more. They felt violated. Connor, the president, did nothing. He felt confident that Anthony would get it handled.

Anthony asked all the employees to bring in copies of their employment contracts because he couldn't find them in the files. Guess what? No one actually had an employment contract under the prior CPO's regime. Anthony didn't trust the employees to properly report their earned vacation days, so there was a stalemate—all vacations frozen, no remedy in site.

Ironically, in the midst of all this turmoil, Anthony had a family emergency and didn't come into the office for a week. No progress was made on the vacation issue during his absence. A few managers let their employees go on vacation anyway, ignoring the vacation freeze. Some managers abided by the freeze, which created inconsistency in the organization and more anger.

When Anthony came back, he was very tan. Hmmm. Folks were questioning whether he indeed had a family emergency—looked like he had a vacation emergency. Since there was still no solution to the vacation day records, Anthony announced that all employees would have fourteen days of vacation. Period. The long-timers, some with thirty days of vacation or more, were livid. Anthony's response to all of this was, "Deal with it."

Connor went along with Anthony's decision, without any consequences.

Coda: I blame this on the CEO. He had blinders on and was too trusting. And he obviously didn't care about his staff. You just don't mess around with people's vacation time.

Computer Games

Cristela had worked for three years at a biotech company with a high security system. Employees had to scan their ID badges to enter the building, to go from floor to floor, to enter certain labs and to leave the building. The ID badge had their photo, fingerprints and employee number. The employee number was integrated in the HR system as well as the security system.

One day, Cristela went online to the employee benefits site to check on her 401(k)-plan progress. When she entered her employee number, she was rejected. She tried several times and couldn't get in the system. She e-mailed HR and was told her number wasn't valid. HR contacted the IT department and they also said that Cristela's number wasn't valid and that in fact, according to the system, she didn't exist. Cristela was confused. She could come and go into high security labs, but she couldn't go online and check her benefits. Go figure. Eventually IT and HR got it together.

Coda: It's amazing, though, how much the little stuff like this can impact the morale and culture.

Board Member Got Played

Adrian had an opening for a training manager. One of the board members said he knew the perfect candidate for the job, Paul. Adrian figured Paul must be good since a board member was backing him. During the interview, there was just something about Paul that didn't feel right to Adrian. He couldn't put his finger on it. When Adrian talked to the board member about his concern that Paul wasn't quite right, the board member was very aggressive in pushing Adrian to hire Paul. So he hired Paul despite a bad feeling in his gut.

Paul started at the bottom of the salary range for the job, making about $40,000, based on his experience. After his first month on the job, Paul asked Adrian for a raise. Adrian was appalled.

Adrian: "No way! Paul, you've only been here for thirty days. You haven't even passed the probationary period and you're still learning the ropes. You're way out of line asking for a raise already."

Paul: "But I'm not making enough money. I made more at my last job. I can't live on this salary."

Adrian: "Dude, that's just too bad. Do your job, prove yourself and in a year when I do your performance review, you'll be considered for a raise."

Paul: "Well can you loan me five bucks? I need money to ride the bus home."

Adrian: "Really? You don't have five dollars? I don't even know what to say to you."

Well you may think this story is crazy, but it gets worse. A couple of months later, Adrian got a call from the state's unemployment office. It turns out that Paul was collecting unemployment checks, while being employed. He had neglected to inform the state when Adrian hired him. So Paul was getting paid in more ways than one. (Yet he didn't have five dollars to ride the bus?)

The board member who recommended Paul was pretty surprised.

Coda: *I'd be very careful about pushing for someone to be hired that I didn't know from first-hand experience. And you need to do a background check, no matter what.*

You've Got to Look the Part

Myla was one of the most well regarded senior account managers with her agency. She'd become a mentor to many of the younger, newer account managers in her department. Vanessa, a junior account manager who'd been with the company for two years, approached Myla:

Vanessa: "Hey Myla, can I talk for a minute in private?"

Myla: "Sure thing, what's up?"

Vanessa: "I really admire how you've managed to grow in your career here. I want to know how I can get bigger accounts and become a full account manager, and eventually to senior, like you. I thought I would be promoted by now. What do I need to do?"

Myla: "Do you really want my straight answer? You may not like what I have to say."

Vanessa: "Yes. I really do. I've heard you are a no B.S. person, Myla. Just tell me."

Myla: "Well, it's not meant to be personal, but here it is. You need to lose weight and dress better. And you need to be more serious in the office. People, mostly upper management, see you as "the funny fat girl." They don't take you seriously. It's just a reality that the game in this business is fifty percent about how you present yourself, fifty percent the quality of your work. I hear your work is good, but I don't think you're going to get assigned to the bigger, high profile accounts and I don't think you're going to get promoted, unless you change your looks and personality. I also don't think that's fair to you, but it's the game around here. I believe people should be themselves and find a place that accepts who they are. So if you choose to stay, you have to play the part… all the way."

Vanessa: "Oh wow. Uh…thanks. I guess. That did hurt more than I expected. But I respect your opinion. Let me think about what you said."

Myla: "If there's some other way I can help you, let me know. I just didn't want to mislead you. The game around here is not just how good you are, it's also how good you look when you're doing it."

Now I expect some of you will think that Myla was very harsh, insensitive and out-of-line. Well, read on…

About three months after this conversation occurred, Vanessa left the company. She went into a different industry within the profession and became highly successful. She didn't lose weight. She didn't lose her sense of humor at work.

Some years later, Myla and Vanessa ran into each other at a professional event.

Vanessa: "I was hoping I'd see you at this event. I wanted to tell you how much I appreciated that conversation we had years ago when I was at the agency working with you. You changed my life. I realized a lot of things about myself and I've made decisions that fit who I am. I will always be grateful to you for your straight talk."

Myla: "Damn. Well, I'm so glad to hear that because I didn't feel good about telling you and I was sure you would hate me forever!"

Coda: Surprised you all...bet you didn't see that half-court shot going in the basket! In this case, the catcher sent a direct signal that was hard for the pitcher to accept, but it worked out. If you can speak from a good place, direct talk is a good thing. How you look and how you behave matters a lot in some workplaces.

You Will Call Me Doctor

Sabina had just completed her Ph.D. in history and was awarded a one-year fellowship at a very prestigious museum. Raymond, a flamboyantly gay African American, was assigned to train and supervise Sabina. Raymond had a bachelor's degree in cultural studies and had worked for the museum for several years. From day one, Raymond was a little too comfortable sharing his love life and talking about his personal issues with Sabina. She didn't like how he could act so familiar and street with her when he had just met her. Sabina, now Dr. Sabina, was only twenty-eight years old, but she knew that even though she was also African American, it was important to keep it professional at work

Raymond: "Girlfriend, you spend way too much time in the museum giving private tours. You need to stay here in the office and write more proposals. I know your office isn't as fabulous as mine, but keep your ass in your chair and work, honey!" (Snapping his head and fingers in that special way.)

Sabina: "Ok, I hear you."

So Sabina spent more time in the office for the next few weeks, turning out multiple proposals, none of which met Raymond's standards.

Raymond: "Your work is terrible. I thought because you had a Ph.D., sister, you would know what you are doing."

Ouch. Sabina was stunned. She wasn't a hundred percent confident that her proposals were on point because she was new at the role, but she also knew her work was far from terrible. Raymond continued to put her down and make snippy remarks about her and her work.

Raymond: "Girl, those dreads you're wearing have got to go. You need to step up your look."

Really? Ok, this was getting way too personal. One day Sabina ran into the head curator at the museum who was surprised to Sabina looking beat down.

Head Curator: "Dr. Sabina. What's wrong? When you started a few weeks ago you were so full of energy and now you look like something has taken the wind out of your sails."

Sabina: "Well, I don't mean to complain, but Raymond is making it very hard for me to work here. He keeps telling me my work isn't good enough and yet he hasn't given me any constructive feedback on how I could do better. I haven't even seen what you all consider a good proposal so I can work towards your style of writing."

Head Curator: "Well, I can fix that. Come with me to my office."

The head curator hands Sabina a proposal to read. Guess what? It was a proposal that Sabina had written, but with Raymond's name on it. She was pissed. She confronted Raymond and they had a big fight—cuss words flying. It was ugly. Raymond was using her work and dissin' her, the S.O.B.! She went to the head curator and told her everything.

Head Curator: "Listen. You are a fellow here with a Ph.D. You don't have to work for Raymond. You can write your own work plan. And you certainly don't have to put up with his behavior."

So Sabina went to Raymond, flipped him off and smiled:

Sabina: "I'm moving to a better office, going to do better work and if you see me, you call me Dr. Sabina in the future, bitch!"

Coda: Don't get it twisted brothers and sisters. Just because we're the same skin color doesn't mean we're all good.

Just Shut Up Already

The head of sales, Gary, was quite the talker and very outgoing, as one would expect from a person in that role. The thing is, Gary talked a lot and was annoying to everyone in the office, including his manager. Gary talked on the phone incessantly, and not just about business. In company meetings, he dominated the time because it took him a long time to make his points. A few of Gary's clients also complained to the head of the company, Kyle, that Gary talked too much. Clearly, Gary wasn't a good listener because he was too busy talking or thinking about what he was going to say next. Kyle tried to coach Gary on this issue to no avail. So Kyle decided to hire an executive coach to help Gary with his excessive chatter.

The coach met with Gary six times to work on being sensitive to listening more and being more concise. Gary seemed to understand that he had a problem and was willing to work on it with the coach. One of tools the coach gave Gary was a set of little plastic sand timers—one minute was blue, two minutes was yellow and three minutes pink—so that he could practice shortening his speaking. The coach also had Gary learn to "count to five" after someone else spoke before he spoke and to clarify and confirm what the speaker had said before speaking.

Gary seemed to improve for a little while, at least in the office. He actually used the sand timers on his desk and in meetings. Everyone in the office teased him about the timers, but they were glad to see him use them. After a few weeks, Gary reverted to his old behavior—talking a lot, saying nothing, and not listening much. One client called Kyle and threatened to leave the business if he didn't get a different sales person; he couldn't stand Gary's yakking. Kyle decided to check with the other clients and prospects on Gary's list. It turns out that many of the prospective clients said the reason they didn't sign on with the company is that they were turned off by Gary's style and quite a few of the existing clients admitted they had learned to tolerate Gary's yakking but didn't like it.

Kyle was determined to keep working with Gary, despite his impact on the business. Eventually Gary quit and went to work for some unsuspecting company. Gary is still known to talk people's ears off.

Coda: Sometimes, old habits are impossible to change.

Textual Harassment

Sarah was in the middle of a bad breakup with her boyfriend, texting emotional messages back and forth in the middle of the night. In the midst of this, she gets a text from her boss. You know what's about to happen.

Sarah, to her boyfriend Evan: I've had it with your bs

Evan: I'm so over your neediness

Sarah's Boss: Hey remember to bring the projector to the client meeting tomorrow.

Sarah: I hate you. we're done. Don't text me you loser.

Sarah's Boss: I'm sorry to bother you so late. My bad.

Sarah: Oh no. That wasn't meant for you. So sorry. I was breaking up with my boyfriend.

Sarah's Boss: Ok. Good to know.

Coda: Be very careful switching between those text conversations.

Smoking & Watching TV

Grace worked as a supervisor for a health care claims processing company that typically hired college grads on a production-based claims processing schedule. The company processed thousands of claims daily, so they would hire processors, take them through a training course and expect them to accurately crank out hundreds of claims each day. Well, they hired a guy; let's call him Frank. Frank passed the training course with flying colors. No issues. He made it through the probationary phase, also without any issues, which was great. Then he started to slack off, not meeting his daily claims quota.

Grace began to closely monitor Frank and found he was taking a 15-minute break every hour to go outside and smoke. She had to write him up and informed him that he was not meeting his quota. The company did not care how many smoke breaks he took, he just needed him to meet his daily quota. Frank promised that he would improve. About a week went by with no improvement to his production. Grace happened to come in one Monday morning on the elevator and saw Frank carrying his personal laptop.

Grace: "What do you plan on doing with that laptop, Frank?"

Frank: "I'm tired of missing my TV shows and I didn't want to get in trouble for using the company laptop."

Coda: Between the numerous smoking breaks and watching TV at his desk, Frank's productivity continually decreased. Frank was terminated.

Game Got Switched

Michaela was a twenty-one-year-old young lady in her third job since high school so she didn't have a lot of work or life experience. She worked at a bakery that was part of a national chain. When Michaela got her first paycheck, she realized she'd been paid twice the amount she'd actually earned. She asked Logan, her region manager, what she should do.

Logan: "Don't worry about it. Just keep it. Too bad HR made a mistake. They'll contact you if they figure it out."

Michaela: "Uh, ok, cool!"

Of course Michaela spent the money—it was more money than she had ever had at one time. She didn't think anything of it. A couple of months went by, so she figured it was an oversight and she'd never hear about it. Well, a new controller was hired at the national office and he immediately found the error. Michaela had to pay the money back to the company through payroll deductions over her next two paychecks. Michaela wasn't happy about it, but thankfully she still lived at home with her parents and could survive the temporary loss of income.

Ironically, by the end of the year, the controller left the company, embezzling thousands of dollars from the bakery company on his way out. Eventually, he was caught and forced to pay the money back—but not through payroll deductions.

Coda: *Honesty really is the best policy.*

You Can't Touch Me

The HR department of a company with forty employees decided to bring in an organization development consultant, Sebastian, to do an assessment of employee morale. Sebastian set up a thirty-minute interview with each of the forty employees, with the same two simple questions: 1) what is going well in the workplace? and 2) what is not going well? After interviewing twelve employees on the first day, Sebastian was surprised that most of the people were consistently mentioning the same person, Mia, with regard to question #2—what's not going well. He figured that maybe he got all of the "Mia haters" on day one.

On day two, about half of the employees interviewed mentioned Mia as a problem. The "Mia" story was consistent—she was arrogant, rude, mean, foul-mouthed and controlling. Mia was a workplace bully. Once all of the employee interviews had been completed, Sebastian sat down with the executive team to give a verbal report of his findings. He outlined all of the consistent themes—both good and bad. In the bad category he reported that the number one issue was the behavior of Mia, the logistics manager. Mia had managed to set a negative tone of fear and animosity with almost everyone that Sebastian interviewed. Some employees came to the interview prepared with printed out copies of ugly e-mails from Mia, to prove their point to Sebastian.

The executive team looked at each other, like this was no surprise. The president of the company laughed and said, "Oh yeah, we knew that." Sebastian said, "Well then why is she still here? Why did you waste your money on me?" To which the president replied, "We can't fire her. She's the best person in her role that we've ever had. She gets a lot done and she knows the system better than anybody. Folks just need to stop hating on Mia and get their jobs done. Mia stays." The VP of HR didn't say a word.

Sebastian left shaking his head….

Coda: *Obviously productivity outweighed civility here.*

Me, Me, Me

Iris was the CEO of a biotech start-up that was quickly rising to fame. At the annual industry conference in Las Vegas, she was asked to introduce the keynote speaker, Dr. Rashad, who had traveled from Sweden. Dr. Rashad was paid $20,000 for his one-hour speaking engagement—that's how high up the food chain he was. Iris approached the podium in the conference center auditorium and proceeded to talk about her start-up company and her personal journey from a being a foster child to getting her Ph.D. to starting the biotech company and how hard she had struggled as a woman. Iris talked on and on about all her accomplishments, all of the famous people she'd met along the way, and how many awards she had won for her ground-breaking research in her field. She cut into Dr. Rashad's time by thirty minutes. Of course, Dr. Rashad didn't care because he was getting paid regardless. The audience was grumbling at the end. No one could believe that Iris could be so self-centered and insensitive to the audience and to the guest speaker, Dr. Rashad.

Coda: Some people think the world revolves around them. They leave little oxygen for others to breathe.

Culturally Clueless

Abby was a marketing coordinator at a small U.S. branch of a European promotion company. She was African American, in her thirties and very professional in appearance and approach to the work environment. Abby's colorful head wraps defined her style and really complimented her outfits well. One day, her boss, Mateo, thought he was being funny.

Mateo: "Hey Abby, what's under those scarves you wear every day? Is Lord Voldemort* hiding in there? Ha, ha!"

Abby didn't think this was funny at all.

*Lord Voldemort is a fictional character in J.K. Rowling's series of Harry Potter novels. Voldemort is the archenemy of Harry Potter.

Coda: This is an example of a microaggression. You don't say *things like that to a woman, especially an African American woman. Her boss was insensitive, politically incorrect, and an idiot.*

Office Party

Rita went to her first office holiday party, after being with the company for just six months. She had a great time! Or as best she could remember, she did. She somehow made it home in a taxi and the next morning, she had to remember where she had left her car. Oh yeah, it was at the bar where the office party had been. She worried that maybe she had gotten carried away, as she was prone to drink a lot. But the next day at work, no one mentioned anything so she figured she was safe. Whew!

Fast forward, six months later, it's time for Rita's one-year performance review. She sits down with her manager and hears that she is meeting the expectations of the job. Just as she was walking out of the review meeting, relieved, her manager calls her back in.

Manager: "Sit down, Rita. There's one more thing. We feel you need to get some serious counseling about your alcohol problem. Maybe you should go to rehab. At the holiday party, your behavior was outrageous, really over the top, and you can't keep going on like that. We were all very afraid for you."

Turns out, Rita was not in the clear after all.

Coda: The manager should have given Rita the feedback about her embarrassing behavior right after the party, not six months later.

Two Truths and a Lie

Five new employees started at the company and were meeting with their new manager on day one. As a warm up, the manager suggested playing a game, to get to know one another.

Manager: "So everyone go around and tell two true things about yourself and one thing that's not true. Then the rest of you try to guess which of the three statements is a lie."

So everyone went around playing this game, telling little stories about their childhoods, or making up things. Then the last person, Sheila, told three stories including this one:

Sheila: "My parents got divorced and now my mom is about to marry my dad's brother, my uncle."

Everyone sat in silence. It was such a bizarre thing to say to a bunch of strangers—your new workmates. Bet you thought this was the lie? It wasn't.

Coda: Too much very disturbing information for the first meeting, my friends.

Figure It Out

Alan was head of sales and Ava worked in operations for a small company. Alan had been harassing Ava at work because she wouldn't go out with him. Everyone in the office knew this was going on, including the boss, Olivia. When Ava had enough of Alan's behavior, she went to Olivia to complain.

Ava: "Olivia, I am sick and tired of all these e-mails from Alan. He keeps badgering me just because I won't go out with him."

Olivia: "Why don't you and Alan leave early today, go to a bar, have a drink and work it out."

Olivia and Alan were friends so Olivia didn't want to chastise him for his behavior. Ava left the company as soon as she found a new job. In this case, there was no HR department to turn to for help.

Coda: *Can you spell "sexual harassment suit"? Really scary but not uncommon in a small business with no HR department.*

Try to stay calm. This stuff really does happen. It's not possible to teach or train someone to be a good person or to use common sense. I hope you will take away something that is real, something that will make you feel better. At least you will find that someone is in way worse shape than you are! I hope it will help you stay sane.

I've continued to be a big reader since childhood. Many books have helped me and continue to help me survive in my journey through the office games. Here are some books and websites I've found valuable in my work as a business consultant. I hope you'll see value in these resources and that you continue to explore ways to function in the work place, whether you plan to be good or bad!

Resources

Agrawal, Miki. *Do Cool Sh*t: Quit Your Day Job, Start Your Own Business, and Live Happily Ever After.* HarperBusiness, 2015.

Bernstein, Albert. *Emotional Vampires at Work: Dealing with Bosses and Coworkers Who Drain You Dry*, Revised and Expanded 2nd Edition. McGraw-Hill Education, 2013.

Foster, Jody J. with Michelle Joy. The Schmuck in My Office: *How to Deal Effectively with Difficult People at Work.* St. Martin's Press, 2017.

Fugere, Brian, Chelsea Hardaway, and Jon Warshawsky. *Why Business People Speak Like Idiots: A Bullfighter's Guide.* Free Press, 2005.

Gladwell, Malcolm. *Blink: The Power of Thinking Without Thinking.* Back Bay Books, 2007.

Gladwell, Malcolm. *The Tipping Point: How Little Things Can Make a Big Difference.* Back Bay Books, 2002.

Harlan, Danielle. *The New Alpha: Join the Rising Movement of Influencers and Changemakers Who Are Redefining Leadership.* McGraw-Hill Education, 2016.

Heath, Chip, and Dan Heath. *Switch: How to Change Things When Change is Hard.* Crown Business, 2010.

Knight, Phil. *Shoe Dog.* Scribner, 2016.

Kouzes, James M. and Posner, Barry Z. *The Leadership Challenge: How to Make Extraordinary Things Happen in Organizations.* Jossey-Bass, 2012.

Lencioni, Patrick. *The Five Dysfunctions of a Team: A Leadership Fable.* Josey-Bass, 2002.

Leonard, Kelly and Tom Yorton. *Yes, And: How Improvisation Reverses "No, But" Thinking and Improves Creativity and Collaboration—Lessons from The Second City.* HarperBusiness, 2015.

Mandel, Debra. *Your Boss is Not Your Mother: Eight Steps to Eliminating Office Drama and Creating Positive Relationships at Work.* Agate B2 2006.

Manson, Mark. *The Subtle Art of Not Giving a F*ck: A Counterintuitive Approach to Living a Good Life.* HarperOne, 2016.

Paton, Cassie. "Five Types of Corporate Culture: Which One Is Your Company." https://blog.enplug.com/5-types-corporate-culture

Porath, Christine. *Mastering Civility: A Manifesto for the Workplace.* Grand Central Publishing, 2016.

Scott, Susan. *Fierce Conversations: Achieving Success at Work & in Life One Conversation at a Time.* Berkley (reprint) 2004.

Sirota. Marcia. "The Difference Between Being Nice and Being Kind." https://qz.com/242637/the-complete-guide-to-swearing-at-work/

Sutton, Robert. *The No Asshole Rule: Building a Civilized Workplace and Surviving One That Isn't.* Business Plus, 2010.

The Ridiculous Business Jargon Dictionary. "The Office Life." http://www.theofficelife.com/business-jargon-dictionary-A.html

Useem, Michael. *The Leadership Moment: Nine True Stories of Triumph and Disaster and Their Lessons for All Us.* Crown Business, 1999.

Wolverson, Roya. "The Complete Guide to Swearing at Work." https://qz.com/242637/the-complete-guide-to-swearing-at-work/

Shout Outs to My Support System

Much love to all who held me up through the process of writing my first book. It was scary and hard and I couldn't have done it without the support of each and every one of you!

Nico—who inspired me to write this book, trusting me to guide him in his business career and making sure I kept this book real and relevant.

Mickey—my loving husband who has been there for me through all my years of corporate life and who gave me the freedom to write this book.

Allison—my beautiful, creative, straight-shooting daughter who keeps me centered and advised me on the book art.

Karin—my fire starter, who kicked me in my butt and told me to "write the damn book already!"

Susan—my funny, smart, no-nonsense sister-friend who gave me great stories and comments and cheered me on to the finish line.

Brian & Jill—who gently pushed me to make a big departure and turn this into a helpful book instead of a series of negative stories.

Kyle & Chad—my educators, who taught me what I needed to know about entering the world of publishing and who championed my idea when it was just a tiny seed.

Larry—who told me straight up that my book was too foul-mouthed and that I needed to tone it down so more people would get my message without being offended.

Molly —for your willingness to read one of my many drafts.

Julian Gaines—the gifted young African American artist and friend who created my cover and interior images with soul, intelligence, and verve.

Julianne Couch—my editor who put up with my irreverent language and held me together when I faltered and became "my sister" in spirit.

Kirk Thomas—the talented layout artist who designed my book cover, expertly guided me through the final process and shared his wonderful sense of humor with me.

Karin—my fire starter, who kicked me in my butt and told me to "write the damn book already!"

Karen M.—my BFF who gave me the gift of her anal attentive skills (yes I meant to say that!) in doing the final copy edit.

Susan—my funny, smart, no-nonsense sister-friend who gave me great stories and comments and cheered me on to the finish line.

And to all my colleagues and friends who shared their stories, you fueled the interesting parts of this vehicle.

Bio

Tanya Rhone is a business consultant and author who has lived and worked in diverse corporate settings and environments. Her childhood in LA's Watts neighborhood gave her a front row seat to the social upheaval of the 1960s. Learning to adapt was the biggest skill she mastered from her youth and that skill propelled her to survive and succeed in corporate America.

Realizing what a college education could do for her future Rhone earned an MBA and worked for major companies: The Clorox Company, Weyerhaeuser, Paragon Trade Brands and Starbucks. Then she started her own consulting practice working with companies and other organizations on strategic planning, organization development, change management, and much more. Now she has written a book in order to share what she's learned about corporate life: not just the ideal workplace it could be, but the sometimes treacherous and always shifting interpersonal environment it often is. During her career, Rhone observed many office environments where people were acting badly at work. She learned that bad behavior and bad decision-making are equal opportunity afflictions: all races, ages, genders, and organizations are susceptible.

Made in the USA
San Bernardino, CA
17 September 2017